Increasi   ishop Burton
A Guide to Qu

Managing Colleges Effectively Series

General Editor: Desmond Keohane

Increasing Effectiveness:
A Guide to Quality Management

John Stone

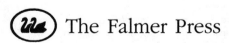 The Falmer Press

(A member of the Taylor & Francis Group)
London • Washington, D.C.

UK   Falmer Press, 1 Gunpowder Square, London, EC4A 3DE
USA   Falmer Press, Taylor & Francis Inc., 1900 Frost Road, Suite 101,
        Bristol, PA 19007

First published in 1997

**A catalogue record for this book is available from the British
Library**

ISBN 0-7507-0717-8 paper

**Library of Congress Cataloging-in-Publication Data are
available on request**

Jacket design by Caroline Archer

Typeset in 10/12 pt Garamond by
Graphicraft Typesetters Ltd., Hong Kong.

*Printed in Great Britain by Biddles Ltd., Guildford and King's Lynn on
paper which has a specified pH value on final paper manufacture of
not less than 7.5 and is therefore 'acid free'.*

Contents

Acknowledgments

My thanks go to the management and staff at Swindon College whose comments, observations, ideas and encouragement have in large measure shaped the systems and approaches detailed here.

In particular I should like to thank:

- Clive Brain, Principal, for his support and permission to adapt and reproduce extracts from a range of college documentation including:

  The Swindon College Charter
  College Service, Teaching and Course Design Standards
  Team Review and Customer Satisfaction Documentation

- Margaret Hawksley and the Curriculum Consultants for permission to reproduce Teaching and Course Design Standards;
- David Saunders and the Marketing and Business Development Team for their contribution to the development of the Franchising Quality Audit.

Introduction

The management of quality has emerged as a key development issue for education in the 1990s and beyond. It has joined growth and efficiency as a core aim for a sector increasingly recognized as a keystone of economic, personal and social well-being.

Everyone is in favour of quality. But when it comes to deciding what quality is, let alone how it is best achieved, there is far less agreement. In many quarters the whole idea of quality management is viewed with considerable suspicion, an understandable view when one recognizes the considerable shift in emphasis which has taken place from the traditional view of quality as an institutional ethos built on the independent and private concern of each individual professional, to a process which is systematically managed, often by outside agencies with widely differing agendas.

There are, however, few stakeholders in the education process who do not argue for 'quality' defined according to their own particular perspective. They include:

- professional organizations — who may choose to emphasize the importance of resources;
- managers who may place more importance on performance;
- government agencies which increasingly assess the achievement of outcomes;
- awarding bodies whose interests are served by the perceived standard and currency of their qualifications.

Other pressures have come from the 'customers' of the education process, particularly students, parents and employers. They increasingly expect higher standards from service providers throughout the public and private sectors, an expectation fuelled by high profile initiatives such as the Citizen's Charter.

Schools and colleges have increasingly turned to industrial and commercial models in their search for quality improvement, but also find themselves having to address more traditional approaches such as inspection.

In the context of education, 'quality' is an elusive concept. It is difficult to define and subject to widely differing interpretations. This book will not seek to map out a unique path to achieving quality. It will not seek to be prescriptive, even though I may reveal personal prejudices along the way drawing, from time to time, on experience and systems developed in Swindon College, where I have had responsibility for this area for some time. Although written from a further education perspective I hope that much of what is described here will also be of interest to schools. It aims to provide a fund of practical ideas and suggestions and help the reader to choose between them in line with their own particular problems, needs and inclinations. There is a seemingly infinite number of possible approaches. You will need to determine the best for you and your institution and then get on with it. This book aims to help.

Chapter 1

Definitions of Quality

Only two weeks ago we handed out a questionnaire to all our students in which we asked 'roughly speaking would you say that on the whole you were pretty happy with the way things were going on the course'. We had several replies and I was delighted to be able to tell the VC that the customer verdict was roughly speaking, 'yes'. (Laurie Taylor, *The Higher*, 1 October 1993)

With so many conflicting views as to what quality is, and how we might recognize it when we see it, I intend to start by attempting to define what might be meant by the term. We might then be in a better position to decide the best way in which we can go about achieving it. I shall consider three broad approaches centering on: (i) customers; (ii) standards; (iii) professional assessment.

Customer-centred Definitions

Customer-centred definitions are widely adopted throughout industry and commerce and are increasingly used throughout the public services. They imply that customer perception is the key to understanding quality with the concept defined subjectively in terms of the customer's opinion of the product or service offered.

Definitions such as:

- satisfying existing and future customer requirements;
- delighting the customer;
- meeting customer requirements.

fall into this class.

Here the aim of the product or service and the staff who provide it is to create customer satisfaction, and quality is delivered when this is achieved.

If you are considering adopting this approach you may wish to consider the following:

- Quality is relative to customer expectations. It can be achieved in a 100-seat lecture theatre or in a 'one to one' tutorial. It may be perceived in dictated notes or a glossy course manual. Everything hinges on what the customer expects.

- Evidently 'quality', under this definition, is not necessarily linked to the level of resources.
- The notion of keeping the customer satisfied sits comfortably with a market driven approach. Your most effective sales team are your satisfied customers.
- 'Customers' are empowered. They have an economic value to the institution and provide the income which pays the staff. Their position in the teaching-learning partnership is therefore strengthened.
- The idea of the student as customer mirrors the reality of existing funding mechanisms where money follows the student.
- The deliberate use of a customer-centred model will contribute to cultural change within the institution.

On the other hand:

- Professional staff are not always comfortable with the term 'customer'. It may alienate them and reduce their commitment to the quality assurance programme.
- Disturbing the relationship between teacher and student may produce negative effects.
- The identification of the customer in education is not at all straightforward. Is it the student we seek to satisfy? How important are the parents in this equation? What about sponsoring employers or other funding agencies?

It may be best to leave the identification of the customer in the hands of the staff team. The process of deciding who the customer is will be valuable in itself, while the most appropriate answer will vary according to the individual circumstances. A question they could seek to answer is 'who is it in our interests to keep happy?'

The notion that professionals are in business to provide unchallenged wisdom to their grateful disciples is in full retreat across all the professions as customer expectations and demands for accountability increase and while sources of advice and information proliferate. The 'levelling up' of roles within the classroom is in itself a significant force behind the current changes in teaching and learning styles.

The linking of quality to customer expectations has been criticized on a number of grounds. What, for example, if the customer chooses to specify 'cheap and nasty' products?. In educational terms what about the student who appears perfectly happy to be left alone, makes no effort and presumably ultimately fails the course? Would the college be able to claim it had delivered a quality service?

It makes more sense to focus on the customer's perception of the quality of the whole learning experience. Quality learning is often the result of an effective partnership between teacher and learner. These partnerships are relatively long-lasting and during that time the expectations of the student will change. Indeed it is the responsibility of education to raise the sights and expectations of individuals. There is considerable scope in this process for the role of the professional to develop in the learner a heightened but realistic set of expectations so that they leave the institution, not feeling they were abandoned to their own worst instincts, but that the time they had invested in the experience was worthwhile.

Standards Centred Definitions

An alternative approach can be seen in the attempts to define quality in terms of an objective framework of pre-determined standards or written specifications. Examples include:

- fitness for purpose and consistently meeting specification;
- the ability to satisfy stated or implied needs;
- conformance to requirements.

Examples of this approach in education include:

- the specification of output competences in NVQ;
- achievement targets.

The advantages of this approach include:

- they provide clear measurable goals for the organization;
- targets can be set and progress measured;
- they can often be expressed in terms of performance indicators;
- quality targets to be set in excess of immediate customer expectations;
- attention is focused on outputs;
- it is easier to monitor outputs than processes.

The disadvantages include:

- complex activities, such as education, may not be adequately described in terms of outputs;
- concentration on achieving targets may distract attention away from other important processes;
- targets can be both motivating and demotivating depending on the circumstances and the individuals involved;

- quality standards in education tend to be professionally rather than customer driven;
- they are less flexible that the customer driven model, particularly as the customer's view changes as a result of the educational process itself.

Professional Assessment

The traditional mechanism for quality management in education, that based on inspection, continues as an important feature in quality assessment today. This is in spite of a general trend in industry and commerce to dispense with inspection in favour of total quality management approaches.

The notion that 'quality cannot be inspected in' may be increasingly accepted outside industry, but this view has not dominated thinking within education. Sir William Stubbs, former Chief Executive of the Further Education Funding Council, in a keynote speech to college principals at the ACFHE annual general meeting in February 1993 laid out his belief that, 'There is no substitute for . . . the scrutiny of what is being provided by a group of experts external to the organization'.

This approach led directly to the formation of the Further Education Funding Council (FEFC) Inspectorate who themselves share many common features with their predecessors, Her Majesty's Inspectorate. This approach is mirrored in Wales, Scotland and the school sector where the National Inspectorates and Office for Standards in Education (OFSTED) perform a similar role.

The survival of the inspection model in education, and the political support on which it depends, centres on the need to provide transparent accountability for public funds and reassurance to the wide range of stakeholders in the education system. There have, however, been changes.

In line with the growing importance attached to numerical indicators and framework criteria, the FEFC Inspectorate differs from its predecessor in that inspectors are expected to comment on a range of published criteria which are summarized in the FEFC Circular *Assessing Achievement* (Circular 93/28), the main categories are as follows:

- responsiveness and range of provision;
- students' recruitment, guidance and support;
- teaching and the promotion of learning;
- students' achievement;
- quality assurance;
- resources (staff, accommodation and equipment).

Each area is graded according to the balance of strengths and weaknesses observed from grade 1 which identifies provision which has many strengths and very few weaknesses to grade 5 which has many weaknesses and very few strengths.

In a review of its inspection arrangements (Circular 96/12) the Funding Council confirmed its basic approach but proposed that the framework be amended to become:

the institution and its mission
teaching and learning
students achievements
curriculum areas: Content and organization
support for students
resources
quality assurance
management
governance

The grade descriptors have also been amended while maintaining the five-point scale referred to above.

Expert assessment is not, of course, confined to the Inspectorate. Peer assessment and review, by a mixture of internal and external staff, has long been a feature of quality assurance arrangements in higher education and many colleges have developed their own systems, occasionally in partnership with other agencies, in order to reproduce for themselves elements of the inspection process.

Colleges have also developed their own quality criteria and assessment systems leaving it for teams of staff to identify the exact targets and performance indicators they feel they can realistically achieve. The approach forms a useful bridge between the need to satisfy external stakeholders while avoiding the demotivating aspects which may follow the imposition of unrealistic or insensitive external targets.

The Funding Council frameworks provide a bridge between totally subjective professional assessment and the standards based approaches discussed earlier. As the elements of the assessment framework become more numerous and more detailed and develop to include numerical targets and performance indicators, the assessment process itself moves from peer assessment to audit, where the role of subjective professional judgment is more constrained in the quest for completeness and increasing objectivity.

Examples of this approach currently in use include the TEC Assure systems, the Scottish equivalent Scottish Quality Management System (SQMS) and a range of quality awards such as ISO 9000, 'Investors in People' and the European Foundation for Quality Management Award. Many of these will be discussed later.

The advantages of an assessment-based approach include:

- inspection/assessment concentrates attention on quality issues;
- the results allow a level of comparison between standards in different institutions to be made;

- institutions are held accountable for the standards of service they provide and the use of public funds;
- observations made by trained, experienced outsiders can provide an important new perspective.

The problems associated with this approach include:

- the resources committed to the process may be out of all proportion to the net benefits obtained;
- the process will divert management and staff attention at the expense of other developments;
- the assessments will always be subjective, no matter how detailed the framework criteria;
- attention will focus on the grades;
- the criteria used may not accord with the priorities of the institution concerned;
- management may feel obliged to adopt a style based on inspection and audit against the best interests of the institution;
- inspection tends to remove responsibility for quality assessment and improvement from management and staff towards the inspectors themselves.

This latter point is a particular danger in education where so much of the process is not measurable and dependent on a relationship, that between the staff and the students, which often develops behind the closed doors of the classroom. Much of this is intangible, unmeasurable and unobservable except on an occasional basis. Even this is questionable as any attempt at observation is almost bound to effect the experience itself. In education, any approach which fails to motivate staff to improve quality is almost bound to fail.

Chapter 2

Selecting an Approach

Link to Organizational Strategy

In one sense the choice of definition is only a technical issue. Once the choice is made, however, whether consciously or unconsciously, it will start to define the emphasis of your approach. That emphasis should in turn be determined by what it is you are trying to achieve, in other words the overall strategy of the organization.

Some examples may help to illustrate this point.

College A enrols 30,000 mainly adult students annually, working a catchment area of only 150,000. It has no plans to move into other areas and little to offer the overseas market. The college must attract its students back several times otherwise it will work itself out of a job. It is imperative that its students leave as 'satisfied customers' so that they will be inclined to return, preferably time and time again.

> The situation suggests that customer satisfaction is a critical factor for this college. A definition and approach based on 'satisfying the customer' would seem appropriate.

College B is a small sixth-form college with the bulk of its income based on full-time 'A' level students. It is in strong competition with a local sixth-form which has made considerable headway following the publication of 'league tables' indicating a better performance in terms of 'A' level average points. Despite a modest move into GNVQ the college sees academic work as its core activity for the foreseeable future.

> This suggests that a standards based definition and approach linked to an 'A' level points performance indicator to be appropriate.

It is, of course, most unlikely that one could find a college where the external constraints, not to mention the prevailing college culture, were as simple as those described. They do however serve to illustrate the basic questions:

- what are our strategies for growth and/or development?;
- what are our priorities for quality improvement?;
- what model, therefore, is most appropriate?

The Use of Critical Success Factors

Faced with the large and complex task of improving quality in an education institution the sheer size and scale of the task can appear daunting at first.

- Where should I start?

and

- How should I prioritize?

are two early questions to be resolved.

All around you will see things which need improving. You will think of many things that could be done, all of which seem important and necessary. But there is a limit to what can be achieved without spreading the resources too thinly to gain any discernible effect.

One useful approach is to determine, at management team or elsewhere, those factors which are key to the very survival of the institution. Critical success factors are not things which are just nice to do, fashionable or politically correct. They are key features of your organization on which the viability and even survival of your business depends. If you do not get them right then a spiral of decline will rapidly set in and will soon be apparent to any objective observer.

The pattern of critical success factors will vary from institution to institution according to circumstances and state of development but they might include:

- financial efficiency;
- student recruitment;
- quality outcomes;
- information systems;
- staff motivation;
- flexibility/responsiveness.

Possible quality improvement projects can then be evaluated against the relative contribution they are likely to make to each critical success factor allowing priorities to be set to maximize the effect on the business within the limits of the resources which can be committed to it.

Continuous Improvement

The continuous improvement of quality is a fundamental tenet of many total quality improvement programmes. It seeks to encourage all parts of the organization to evaluate the quality of what they provide and seek to achieve a practical level of improvement over a defined period of time.

It is particularly relevant to organizations, or parts of organizations, which are not likely to be affected by radical change during the planning period. Staff are expected to effect improvements, but the pace and scale of those improvements is very much theirs to decide. Improvement targets can be set by the staff themselves, these targets are therefore owned and supported by the staff who may therefore be more likely to work to achieve them.

There are times, however, when continuous improvement may not be possible or appropriate and 'step change' may be required.

For example:

- changes in staffing, management or structure may be necessary;
- a process may benefit from being redesigned from scratch, rather than marginally improved.

Continuous improvement is a non-threatening yet powerful concept used by many organizations to define their approach to quality improvement. There are times, however when modest improvements are not enough and significant and rapid change may be necessary. In such cases management action may be necessary, as often only management has the power and command over resources necessary to make the necessary changes. *Continuous improvement may need to be supplemented by step change.*

Chapter 3

External Quality Awards

In determining an approach to quality improvement a quality framework can be an invaluable tool. Reference has already been made to the framework, such as that detailed in the Further Education Funding Council Circular (93/ 28), *Assessing Achievement* or alternatively through use of the organization's own critical success factors.

A quality improvement framework:

* provides a series of headings under which possible improvement projects can be determined, classified and prioritized;
* helps to ensure that the quality improvement process covers all important areas of the organization;
* provides a means by which progress can be measured;
* suggests an underpinning philosophy to give intellectual coherence to the quality improvement process.

The choice of framework should again be determined by the organization's overall strategy. The search for an external award can help maintain momentum and management commitment along the long and slow road to quality improvement but it is important that the main features of the award are broadly in line with organizational priorities. Some of the better known frameworks currently in use are described below.

BS 5750

BS 5750, increasingly referred to by its international equivalent the ISO 9000 series, is probably the best known of all quality assurance standards currently on offer. BS 5750 is an industrial model developed from a belief that quality control through random sampling of output could be made more effective by auditing the systems within a supplier designed to assure the quality of the product[1]. The first FE college to achieve the standard was Sandwell College for part II through a Government funded pilot scheme.

BS 5750 is concerned with documenting systems and procedures to ensure they meet certain criteria. It is not concerned with outcomes, the quality of the final product or the learners' experience. At the core of BS 5750 is the National Standard which requires fully documented procedures and processes to be operated at all levels of the organization in the following 20 categories:

- management responsibilities
- quality system
- contract review
- design control
- documentation control
- purchasing control
- customer supplied product
- identification and traceability
- process control
- inspection and testing
- control of inspection and measuring equipment
- inspection and test status
- control of non-conforming product
- corrective action
- handling, storage, packaging and delivery
- quality records
- internal quality audits
- training
- servicing
- statistical techniques

The BS 5750 registration mark is not a product quality kite mark and does not establish a level of excellence for a product. The system does not purport to be anything more than a way of describing the capability of this system to produce goods to specification. As BSI itself points out the company may not always meet all the requirements of its internal system and the 1990 American Society for Quality Control Congress commented, 'The ISO 9000 standard intentionally does not emphasize the ability to demonstrate continual quality improvement capability'. It is, however, equally true that quality cannot be guaranteed without recognized and effective systems in place.

Sandwell estimated the costs involved to be as much as £60,000 for a large college, perhaps not a large sum in commercial terms but a significant sum in the context of more restricted college budgets. Careful cost benefit analysis would need to be undertaken before such a route was followed.

BS 5750 remains, however, the most widely accepted and best known quality assurance standard. It is recognized internationally (ISO 9000) and benefits from rigorous external assessment. A college which has achieved BS 5750 is assured of a comprehensive set of procedures, but there is no guarantee that the organization will live up to its demands.

The Scottish Quality Management System (SQMS)

The Scottish Quality Management System, now widely used throughout Scotland, brings together the main quality systems and guidelines used in Scottish education and training. The resulting standard[2] is, therefore, most comprehensive, addressing as it does the different requirements of:

- the local enterprise companies (LECs);
- Scottish Vocational Education Council (SCOTVEC);
- the Scottish Office;
- IIP Scotland;
- BS 5750.

This results in a fourteen-point standards framework and an audit process which supports the institution's quality improvement programme and defines the requirements of external accreditation.

The SQMS structure is as follows:

- strategic management
- quality management
- marketing
- staffing
- staff development
- equal opportunities
- health and safety
- premises and equipment
- communication and administration
- financial management
- guidance services
- programme design
- programme delivery
- assessment for certification

The strengths of the SQMS system include its coverage of existing standards and its customization for education and training. As with all standards based approaches the questions asked may be too broad for mere audit. For example

Are there effective budgetary control, monitoring and reporting mechanisms?

may seem an innocent enough question, but anyone who has poured over a financial audit report will appreciate that such a question is wide enough to spawn an industry of its own and that the truth of the matter may not be discernible in the context of a quality audit. The breadth itself is a strength but it is also a weakness if the institution is drawn into addressing the full range of issues, without reference to its own development needs.

Investors in People (IIP)

IIP is a national standard developed by the Employment Department, currently being promoted strongly by most Training and Enterprise Councils.

The Government target is for 70 per cent of organizations employing more than 200 people and 35 per cent of organizations employing 50 or more to be Investors in People by the year 2000.

By early 1995 11 per cent of larger organizations had achieved the standard with only 5 per cent of smaller companies making the grade.

IIP is based on a national standard drawn from good personnel practice observed in the country's top companies. The standard encompasses the setting and communicating of goals, developing people to meet these goals and matching peoples' skills to business needs.

The key elements of the framework are as follows:

(i) Commitment
An investor in people makes a commitment from the top to develop all employees to achieve its business objectives.

- The commitment from top management to train and develop employees to communicate effectively throughout the organization.
- Employees at all levels are aware of the broad aims or vision of the organization.
- The organization has considered what employees at all levels will contribute to the success of the organization and has communicated this effectively to them.
- Where representative structures exist, communication takes place between management and representatives on the vision of where the organization is going and the contribution employees (and their representatives) will make to its success.

(ii) Planning
An investor in people regularly reviews the needs and plans the training and development of all employees.

- A written but flexible plan sets out the organization's goals and targets.
- A written plan identifies the organization's training and development needs and specifies what actions will be taken to meet these needs.
- Training and development needs are regularly reviewed against goals and targets at the organization, team and individual level.
- A written plan identifies the resources that will be used to meet training and development needs.
- Responsibility for training and developing employees is clearly identified and understood throughout the organization, starting at the top.
- Objectives are set for training and development actions at the organization, team and individual level.
- Where appropriate, training and development objectives are linked to external standards, such as NVQs and units.

(iii) Action
An investor in people takes action to train and develop individuals on recruitment and throughout their employment.

- All new employees are introduced effectively to the organization and all employees new to a job are given the training and development they need to do that job.
- Managers are effective in carrying out their responsibilities for training and developing employees.
- Managers are actively involved in supporting employees to meet their training and development needs.
- All employees are made aware of the training and development opportunities open to them.
- All employees are encouraged to help identify and meet their job-related training and development needs.
- Action takes place to meet the training and development needs of individuals, teams and the organization.

(iv) Evaluation

An investor in people evaluates the investment in training and development to assess achievement and improve future effectiveness.

- The organization evaluates the impact of training and development actions on knowledge, skills and attitude.
- The organization evaluates the impact of training and development actions on performance.
- The organization evaluates the contribution of training and development to the achievement of its goals and targets.
- Top management understands the broad cost and benefits of training and developing employees.
- Action takes place to implement improvements to training and development identified as a result of evaluation.
- Top management's continuing commitment to training and developing employees is demonstrated to all employees.

(Taken from 'The Revised Indicators', Investors in People UK, 1996.)

Investors in People is based on the assumption that quality is achieved through people, in particular by involving them in the goals of the organization and motivating and supporting them to achieve those goals. It is particularly appropriate in a college environment, where the quality of service is particularly sensitive to the quality of the teaching staff and where the standard itself sets out to promote the importance of supporting and training staff, the business that colleges are in. Colleges may also gain credibility with employers through the achievement an external award.

The Investors in People standard is not, however, staff-centred. People are trained in line with the needs of the business according to clearly expressed business goals. This can imply a considerable cultural shift in educational institutions, a theme which will be explored later.

Investors in People is also criticized as being insufficiently 'customer' centred. Customers should indeed benefit as a result of applying the standard, but the focus, in the first instance is the organization itself.

As with BS 5750, Investors in People addresses itself to one piece, albeit an important one, of the quality management jigsaw. Multifaceted approaches which attempt to analyze the whole problem and move ahead on a number of fronts may be described as 'total quality' approaches.

Notes

1 BS 5750/ISO 9000 (1987) *A Positive Contribution to Better Business*, London, DTI.
2 Scottish Quality Management System, SCOTVEC, Scottish Enterprise, Highland and Islands Enterprise, 1993.

Chapter 4

Total Quality Management (TQM)

Total quality management has grown from the view that quality cannot be 'inspected in' to a product or service. For the adherents of TQM the essential feature of quality improvement is the attitude of the workforce. They must accept responsibility for quality, ensure continuous improvement or simply get it 'right first time'. Quality will improve if the staff of the organization are motivated or inclined to improve it. As such total quality management becomes inseparable from general management practice.

Definitions of TQM

There are many interpretations of the term TQM. Its current prominence owes much to the fascination with Japanese economic success and the approaches to quality adopted by many leading Japanese companies. They, in turn, appear to have been influenced by the activities of the so-called quality gurus such as Deming, Juran, Crosby and Ishikawa, all of whom have developed and often marketed their own personal view as to the essential features of TQM.

Within the TQM debate one can see evidence of the standards versus continuous improvement debate referred to earlier. Crosby (1978) has made most impact with his standards oriented slogan 'Right first time', while Deming's employee-centred approach epitomized the continuous never ending improvement school of thought (Deming, 1986).

Despite their differences the following definitions help to illuminate the what is implied.

Some stress the importance of people:

- TQM is a process of managing and measuring the continuous quality improvement of everything a company does. The process is predicated on the principle that quality begins and ends with shared commitment, attitudes and actions.[1]
- TQM is a philosophy of never-ending improvement achievable only by people.[2]

Some stress the intended impact on the business:

- the management of change to implement the organization's strategic business mission[3] or

- a strategy for improving business performance[4]

whereas others give more prominence to the customer:

- a process of continuous improvement in quality based on the assumption that there is a constant need to adapt services in response to customer needs.

Commonwealth hotels[5] have summarized much of this in a slogan used to promote their TQM commitment internally:

- Total — everyone is involved
- Quality — delight the customer
- Management — organize not supervise

TQM 'Gurus'

Arguably the most influential of all the 'quality gurus' is W Edwards Deming. Deming was first 'discovered' in Japan where he is virtually a national hero. The most important features of his work are contained in his 'fourteen points' which include:

- cease dependence on inspection;
- improve constantly;
- eliminate slogans, exhortations and numerical targets.

His 'deadly diseases' question some of the fundamental tenets of modern management practice, for example: evaluation of performance; management by numerical target.

He also criticizes the emphasis on short-term profits and the mobility of management in Western companies.

Deming's philosophy is underpinned by his use of Statistical Process Control (SPC). At the heart of this lies the statistical observation that all processes, however well controlled, are subject to variation[6].

The variations are due to either: special causes (which are the responsibility of the individual); or common causes (which are caused by the system and therefore can only be rectified by management action).

Joseph Juran (see below) estimates that only 15 per cent of the quality problems in an organization are due to special causes while Deming has revised that figure down to 6 per cent (and more recently 2 per cent) leaving the overwhelming majority of the causes of variation solely within the province of management.

Although there may be disagreement about the relative proportions, the message is clear. Any quality policy which relies on exhortations to the workers to perform better is bound to fail it is does not attack the structural failures in the system which can only be addressed by management, if indeed they can be addressed at all.

Within SPC there are statistical mechanisms for distinguishing between special and common causes provided that sufficient data is available. Hence it can be determined whether a process is in or out of statistical control, i.e. whether the system is performing to its maximum potential and providing minimum variation in the quality of its products.

Among the other 'quality gurus' who have gained a measure of international recognition is Joseph Juran who emphasizes the close linkages between planning, quality and management control. He apparently conflicts with Deming with his emphasis on numerical quality goals, measures and targets.

Philip Crosby has gained an amount of (well marketed) notoriety for his concept of 'right first time'. He accepts that management must set the tone but the emphasis of his message differs from Juran and Deming in that it focuses on the need for improvements at the operational level.

Kaoru Ishikawa is best known as a pioneer of the use of quality circles, groups of workers coming together, on a voluntary basis, to generate ideas for quality improvement in a particular area of activity. Ishikawa is also associated with the promotion of a range of 'TQM tools' including the Ishikawa or 'fishbone' diagram which is used in the analysis of cause and effect relationships.

TQM has the advantage of being flexible in implementation and therefore adaptable to a college's own priorities. This flexibility could prove particularly useful to a college which already has to live up to a range of quality criteria imposed by other stakeholders. It can be implemented gradually building on the strengths of the organization in line with the resources available.

TQM is people centred and particularly suited to services such as education which depends fundamentally on people who are themselves used to a high degree of independence and in many cases suspicious of intrusive administrative systems.

It highlights the importance of the services provided within the organization to the quality of the learning experience and the inter-dependence and common concerns of teaching and non-teaching staff at a time when many colleges are trying to build a corporate view in the aftermath of incorporation. It is also a proven model with something of a track record (particularly in the USA).

The commitment required to sustain momentum, particularly without the encouragement to sustain the effort required over the long term, should not be underestimated. Achieving a climate in which TQM can be achieved is closely allied with the effective management and culture of the organization. As such it cannot be 'installed' without affecting the core processes and assumptions on which the business is run.

A TQM Framework

The British Standards Institution has published a 'standard' against which organizations aspiring to TQM can measure themselves. At present there are no plans for external accreditation along the lines of BS 5750. The standard, known as BS 7850, draws in many of the concepts described above. The sixteen 'elements' listed include a focus on customer satisfaction, empowerment, team work and communication as characteristics of a company successfully operating TQM.

The foundation of TQM lies somewhere between the edicts and often conflicting views of a host of quality gurus and the demonstrable success of international companies who have adapted the approaches, initially pioneered in Japan, to the international setting.

The key concepts can be described as follows:

- *The customer*

Satisfying the customer is at the centre of TQM. That customer can be external to the organization (normally the student) or an internal customer for a product or service provided. Customers are involved in determining needs and setting standards and checks are made to ensure those needs are met.

- *Empowerment and accountability*

The commitment of top managers is essential but quality must be managed at all levels of the system. Authority should be passed to those best able to make decisions and team-work encouraged. As power is devolved accountability for the use of power must move with it.

- *Continuous improvement*

However good a service is, it should always be possible to improve it. Eliminating the costs of failure can mean better quality management can increase resource efficiency.

- *Standards*

Progress towards quality is measured by agreed achievable realistic standards set with reference to customer requirements. The standards should be dynamic, flexible and owned at the point of service delivery.

- *Participation*

TQM philosophy demands commitment and participation. Its implementation concentrates on ensuring that in time all employees are involved in developing techniques to achieve improvement. All staff ultimately pass through a skills training process. TQM in education should include students as partners in the process, including their ideas and efforts in the process of continuous improvement.

- *Planning*

The TQM approach permits colleges to identify those areas in which improvement is critical to its success — so called 'critical success factors'. A phased improvement programme can then be undertaken at an achievable rate consistent with its overall development plan. In this way TQM can embrace a gradualist approach through which interest and acceptance can be built on success rather than promise.

- *Open communication and information systems*

An open and supportive management style combined with an emphasis on good communications to support congruence between corporate and individual attitudes is essential.

- *Quality management systems*

With a reduction in direct management control greater reliance can be placed on quality systems which can give confidence and performance information at all levels and decrease the need for direct intervention and supervision.

- *The use of TQM tools*

A range of tools has been developed to assist in the development and implementation of TQM. The use of statistical process control and the concepts of common and special causes are important in determining levels of accountability in as much as there is no point in making people accountable for factors over which they have no effective control.

Total Quality Awards

The features outlined above are reflected in a number of total quality awards, two of which are described here.

The Malcolm Baldridge Award

The Malcolm Baldridge Quality Awards are made annually to recognize US companies for business excellence and quality achievement. Awards are given in each of three categories: (i) manufacturing; (ii) service companies; (iii) small businesses.

The award ceremony is a high profile affair with awards normally being presented by the President of the United States.

The Baldridge criteria represent one of the longest standing TQM frameworks. They have been developed over time and in 1995 were expressed as follows:

- leadership
- information and analysis
- strategic planning
- human resources development and management
- process management
- business results
- customer focus and satisfaction

The criteria illustrate the comprehensive reach of total quality management directing attention towards core business processes as well as operational systems and results.

The award itself is achieved through a system of scoring against detailed criteria drawn from the Baldridge framework.

The European Foundation for Quality Management (EFQM)

Probably the latest and most comprehensive of all the total quality frameworks, the European Foundation for Quality Management and its British equivalent, the British Quality Foundation Awards, are both gaining ground. Efforts are being made to promote them within the public services and a 'translation' of the standard for education has recently been published.

Like the Baldridge award its requires qualitative assessment, scored against a range of criteria.

A distinctive feature of the EFQM framework is the equal balance between 'enablers' and 'results', effectively implying that total quality is dependent on both process and product.

The key to the process is qualitative 'self-assessment', an attractive feature for organizations wishing to transfer accountability for quality to staff, but concerned at the lack of rigour that this may imply.

The main elements of the framework and their respective weightings are as follows:

Enablers
- Leadership — 10%
- People management — 9%
- Policy and strategy — 8%
- Resources — 9%
- Processes — 14%

Results
- People satisfaction — 9%
- Customer satisfaction — 20%
- Impact on society — 6%
- Business results — 15%

From the point of view of education there are evident advantages in moving to a system of moderated self-assessment. The award itself may not be a realistic goal for many but the process itself may be a useful one provided that it is developed in the context of the institution's own development agenda.

The inclusion of output criteria is, I believe, a positive point. It is all too easy to construct a rational, intellectually powerful quality management system which does not deliver. Many quality frameworks, including some described here, concentrate on internal processes and do not make reference to the effects on the business and its customers. Quality managers need to be haunted by the thought that even the most logical, carefully constructed system may in the wrong circumstances actually harm quality as people lose sight of their goals and fail to find convincing new ones.

Educationalists may also be pleased to see reference to the impact on society amongst the criteria but the relative weighting given to processes (the obvious place to include teaching) and customer satisfaction may not seem appropriate in all cases.

One question to be faced by those seeking to adapt this scheme to the educational environment must be the writing of the process criteria to give adequate emphasis to teaching and learning and whether the model could adequately replace well established processes such as course team review.

Added Value Chains

I have several times sought to underline the importance of aligning a quality system with the overall strategic goals of the organization. In the commercial sector this can be investigated through the use of Porter's value chain which tracks the effect of adding value through the organization's processes.

The educational equivalent of this process suggests an alternative framework which focuses attention on the main purpose of the enterprise, that of adding value to the student throughout his/her association with the institution.

For example:

* understanding community needs
* developing learning opportunities
* publicity and sales
* enquiries and advice
* enrolment and induction
* teaching and learning
* guidance
* assessment
* moving on
* keeping contact

One of the drawbacks of TQM is the scale of its ambitions. In seeking to address the quality improvement needs of everyone and everything it can be painfully slow in a world where management and staff alike are under pressure to achieve and demonstrate results quickly. Focusing on the direct quality of the student experience should certainly accelerate the noticeable effects.

On the other hand lack of attention to the other elements in the 'internal quality chain' may:

- Make it more difficult for the organization to achieve greater efficiency in its administrative overheads.

Lack of attention to these areas can prove costly and not only to the non-teaching side of the organization. Poorly run services soon impact on additional administrative demands for teaching staff with the obvious knock-on effect on the quality of the teaching experience.

- Tend to make it less responsive and accessible to new customer groups.

The prevailing academic culture of many schools and colleges is normally student centred, but this proper professional orientation is sometimes restricted to existing students and traditional customer groups. The activities of a strategic marketing function, the operation of front of house or outreach services or even the inclination of the premises function to create accessible and welcoming environments can be decisive in the search for new markets.

- Reduce further the status and influence of business support staff.

One of the key feature of TQM lies in the drive to reduce artificial distinctions between grades of staff and promote a recognition of the value and interdependence of all members of the organization. There have traditionally been at least two main cultural traditions in education, the dominant academic culture of teachers and lecturers and the bureaucratic culture of the administrative support. Since incorporation there has been a distinct levelling up as contractual terms and conditions converge. Highly qualified professionals have been brought in on the business support side. Overemphasis on teaching and learning without sufficient regard to the factors underlying it slow down this trend.

In practical terms the framework proposed above is sufficiently broad to avoid most of these possible drawbacks. It is however both more focused and less even-handed than some of the more general approaches described earlier.

TQM in Education

There has been considerable interest in the application of TQM type models to educational institutions. In 'Implementing Total Quality Management' the South West Association for Further Education and Training reported on the experience of five further education colleges in the south west. They concluded:

'TQM appears to be particularly suited to enterprises where the main resource is staff, since it particularly emphasises the role of staff. . . . Colleges participating in the project gained a very good practical and theoretical understanding of TQM . . . thus it would appear that TQM is a very good choice of quality management system for further education colleges.'

Mt. Edgecoombe School

One of the most celebrated examples of the application of TQM in an educational environment comes from Mt. Edgecoombe School in Alaska, USA. Mt. Edgecoombe is a residential school of about 200 students from seventeen ethnic groups generally from poor backgrounds.

TQM evolved in the school through adopting TQM strategies at classroom level. Learning is characterized as a partnership between the students and the staff of the school, a partnership in which students and teachers are jointly engaged in the search for continuous improvement in educational standards.

The results claimed are impressive with school graduate unemployment at only 2 per cent against a state average of 25 per cent with high rates of progression to college, low drop out rates and minimal behavioural problems. All in stark contrast to the school's earlier reputation.

The Mt. Edgecoombe experience is particularly interesting as it underlines the importance and benefits of involving students, characterized as partners in the provision of the education service, focusing on TQM as a development which directly rather than indirectly involves students as distinct from working through management and staff.

The importance of customer involvement in TQM, particularly in services such as education where long-term relationships are possible, is not at present well developed in TQM literature.

In addition to endorsing the use of TQM in education, the South West Consortium also favoured Deming's approach over some other contenders. In particular they rejected Crosby's 'right first time' philosophy as less applicable and 'based too much on exhortation' to be entirely credible to academic staff.

Mt. Edgecoombe School has proposed an interpretation of Deming's fourteen points for use in education[7]. They include:

- cease dependence on testing;
- work with the educational institutions from which students come;
- institute education and training on the job for students, teachers, and administrators;
- drive out fear;
- break down barriers between departments;
- eliminate slogans and exhortations.

The Galileo Institute

The application of TQM to educational institutions has something of a track record in the USA. The Galileo Institute, which has worked in this field for some years, supports Deming's principles but believes that they will not work in education. Deming, they point out does not believe in targets and takes a long term view, as much as ten years in some cases. The reality in education, however, revolves around an increasing variety of externally imposed targets in time scales which are seldom more than three years. The situation is even more critical in the USA where college directors are frequently asked to leave if they have not fulfilled expectations within a three-year period.

Galileo is not alone in ascribing part of the success of TQM in Japan to its cultural peculiarities. In particular Japanese society is seen as taking a longer term view with employees generally staying with the same company for all of their working lives. Western societies by contrast are more individualistic and short-term. Galileo therefore stress the need to build TQM through a focus on factors which will produce early results where success will build support and tolerance for a longer term programme. They also highlight the need for conflict management in team building, an acceptance of the importance of dealing with those human factors which can derail the best intentions of even the most carefully constructed scheme.

The Further Education Development Association (FEDA)

The interest in TQM in UK education is not confined to the work in the south west referred to above. The Further Education Development Association and its precursor the Further Education Unit (FEU) has also been active in this field through the FEU publication *Quality Matters*, support for a longer term project looking at the effect of TQM as applied in FE colleges in Stockport and Canterbury (RP 671) and the publication, *Making Quality Your Own* (1995) which suggests the following approach:

- decide what quality means in the College;
- strategically plan and manage for quality improvement;
- operationally plan and manage for quality improvement;
- evaluate.

Ed Sallis and Peter Hingley (1992) have also written on the adaptation of TQM in the context of British Further Education. They support the strong customer focus of TQM but accept that customers in this instance can be very uninformed about the nature of the product and have diverse expectations of what constitutes quality. Quality in education, they propose, can be associated with the reputation of the institution itself. They ask whether an inner city college can ever have a 'quality' reputation.

In this discussion Sallis and Hingley seem to come close to suggesting that 'absolute' quality exists. This is an alluring prospect. After all we all know quality when we see it. Whether we would all agree is another matter. The authors' definition of quality as the delivery of a consistent service to pre-defined standards also indicates the view of quality as an absolute which can be achieved.

I have argued that, in service industries and particularly in education, the customer's view of what constitutes an acceptable standard will develop over time. Hence an absolute standard is unlikely to satisfy customer expectations except for a limited time. Indeed in view of the diversity of expectations that Sallis and Hingley themselves draw attention to it is unlikely to satisfy all customers for any amount of time.

The derivation of quality standards may have its place. They can be useful management tools, they can aid in team building and they can concentrate attention on quality improvement and be used to support benchmarking. They must, in the context on education, be dynamic, flexible and owned by those involved. Above all they must reflect the developing expectations of the service's customers.

As to whether a college dealing with 'students' from deprived backgrounds can ever achieve a quality reputation, the Mt Edgcoombe experience provides positive evidence.

Strategic Quality Management

'Consultants at work' were a group working with six FE colleges in the north west engaged on a TEED (Department of Employment Training and Enterprise Division) funded project aimed at supporting the management of quality improvement in further education. They coined the term 'Strategic Quality Management' which they define as 'The focused effort of everyone in the college to place at the centre of their individual and corporate concerns the needs of the learner'.

Strategic quality management formulates a systematic approach to the management of quality centring on five questions:

(i)   Strategy — how are we intending to achieve our vision?
(ii)   Management capability — what will this demand of our managers?
(iii)   Involvement — how do we gain our staff's commitment to this endeavour?
(iv)   Resources — how do we ensure our resources facilitate our intentions?
(v)   Quality improvement — what will we offer the learners?

Each question is supported by a list of key features which provide a checklist for good practice. Like all checklists they are useful prompts but one cannot say whether they all necessary, sufficient or indeed the right priorities for a given

They are also essentially management centred. They address, to
, the involvement of staff but fall far short of empowerment.

otes

1 *Quality Matters*, FEU, August 1991.
2 Dodds, M. (Ed) (1992) *Implementing Total Quality Management — Case Studies
from Five Further Education Colleges*, SWAFET.
3 Chase, R.L. (Ed) (1993) *Implementing TQM — the Best of TQM Magazine*, IFS
International Ltd.
4 Christopher Jones Management Services (1992) *Total Quality Management and the
Role of Management Services*, November.
5 'The application of quality management principles in education', *Myron Tribus*,
November, 1990.
6 *Why SPC?*, British Deming Association, 1992.
7 Marsh, J. (1992) *Total Quality Improvement in Education*, Avon TEC.

Chapter 5

Getting Started

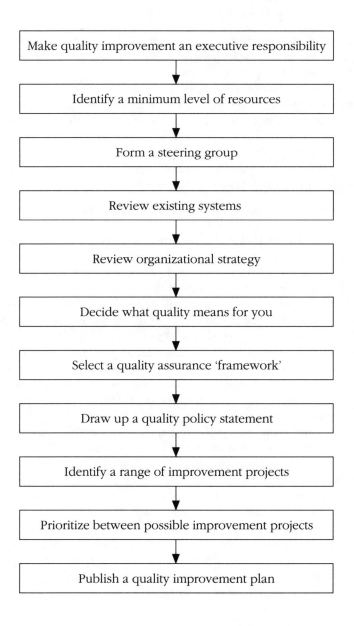

Make quality improvement an executive responsibility

↓

Identify a minimum level of resources

↓

Form a steering group

↓

Review existing systems

↓

Review organizational strategy

↓

Decide what quality means for you

↓

Select a quality assurance 'framework'

↓

Draw up a quality policy statement

↓

Identify a range of improvement projects

↓

Prioritize between possible improvement projects

↓

Publish a quality improvement plan

Quality is everyone's job. It cannot be hived off into a quality department that in some way checks samples and retrieves poor quality. This is particularly true of education because:

- key parts of the processes take place behind closed doors;
- each event is unique;
- student performance depends on a range of factors, many of which are outside the control of the individual teacher;
- inspection is almost bound to distort the process that it seeks to assess.

Can anyone say that their own or their student's behaviour is unaffected when an inspector sits in the back row taking down notes? Does the teacher work 'normally' when an inspector is present?

Quality management will not, however, just happen. It is a complex and difficult process which goes right to the heart of organizational strategy. If it is to be all embracing it will challenge the culture and value systems of the organization. Improvement programmes will need to be driven down throughout all areas of the organization often in the face of studied apathy or outright resistance. Only senior managers in the organization are realistically able to take on this task. Step 1 therefore becomes:

- *Make quality improvement an executive responsibility*

The allocation of resources is also an issue. Should there be a separate budget for quality improvement or for specific quality improvement projects? What level of staffing should the designated senior manager acquire in order to achieve the organization's objectives in this regard?

The answers to these questions will depend on local skills and the attributes and workloads of those involved. I would, however, argue that dedicated resources awarded should be as few as possible.

Quality improvement should be accepted as part of the day-to-day activity of everyone in the organization. This may be best achieved when ongoing quality improvement is integrated with general operation and effected through the existing resources and budgets of the organization. In this spirit the level of staffing should also be minimized. The establishment of a quality assurance function may create the impression that quality improvement is their responsibility, absolving others from their part in the process.

Putting in new systems, however, can be resource intensive and from time to time project funding for the development and installation of a new process may be in order provided that the ongoing operation of this system falls to an established part of the organization. The general rule should be to change agendas and priorities in favour of quality improvement rather than bolt on extra functions. Such an approach may be more difficult to achieve in the short term but if successful the reward will be greater ownership of the system, greater effectiveness and a significant contribution to ongoing cultural change within the organization. In summary:

- *Identify a minimum level of resources*

Although the discrete budgets available may be restricted there will be a considerable resource of interest and expertise available on a voluntary basis throughout the institution. The drawing together of a group of enthusiasts, consciously drawn from all areas and levels of the staff can be one of the most significant features in ensuring a successful programme. The group will:

- bring new ideas and perspectives to the table;
- provide a resource for moving projects and sub-projects on in their own areas;
- ensure consultation and commitment from key areas;
- provide a sounding board for the practicality and acceptability of ideas;
- provide a mechanism for moving the process on and reviewing progress;
- symbolize the commitment of the institution to a broad based and open development programme;
- provide an opportunity for critics to be heard and drawn into the programme at an early stage.

The Steering Group might include:

The Personnel Manager
The Staff Development Officer
The Director of Curriculum
Special Needs Coordinator
Lecturers specializing in quality assurance and related issues
Managers and staff from both teaching and business support teams

Membership should be open to all and periodically refreshed through open invitation. In summary:

- *Form a Steering Group*

You are unlikely to have the benefit of a 'green field site' on which to erect a perfect new quality assurance structure. There will already be many quality improvement mechanisms in operation, lying dormant, or limping along in a state of disrepair at all levels. There may, for example, be perfectly adequate course review or student survey mechanisms operating in pockets throughout the organization. Those who put them together are likely to be committed to them and are therefore making them work. Before launching a new master plan its may be as well to consider what is out there and whether it can be adapted to meet the overall corporate need. Ownership is worth a lot and commitment to a system can overcome many apparent errors in design. The next step should then be to:

- *Review and evaluate existing quality systems and procedures at all levels of the organization*

The next stages have been discussed in detail in chapter 1. The main points being:

- *Review Organization Strategy*

  — What are the main strategic options available to the institution?
  — How does it intend to achieve its mission?
  — Do you seek to grow into new or existing markets?
  — If so what will be important to your customers?
  — What is your market position likely to be?
  — Will you seek to be known primarily as the school or college with the best exam results, the best student experience or as a fun place to learn?
  — In what way will quality assurance assist in this process?
  — What does quality mean to you and to the customers you seek to attract?

After debating these issues you should be in a position to:

- *Decide what quality means to you*

Choosing a definition for quality in line with the discussion in chapter 1 you will decide between

  — Customer focused approaches, or
  — Definitions based on standards and targets

Is quality measured by:

  — Your place in the league table?
  — Your percentage pass rate?
  — Your inspection grades?
  — Your customers' opinions?
  — Your own profession opinion?
  — The results of a self-assessment process?

The choice is yours, but it is important. Whether it is spoken or merely understood, the choice will influence your approach, your priorities and the results of the quality improvement process.

At this stage you should be able to move rapidly towards determining the basis of your whole approach.

It may seem the most daunting and indigestible part of the exercise as you begin to appreciate the enormity and complexity of the exercise you have embarked upon. Take things one step at a time:

- *Select a quality assurance 'framework' and thereby an overall 'philosophy'*

Examples of possible frameworks were described in some detail in chapters 2 to 4. They included:

— ISO 9000
— Investors in People
— Strategic Quality Management
— Total Quality Management
— Added Value Chains
— Malcolm Baldridge Awards
— European Foundation for Quality Management
— Scottish Quality Management System

After weighing up the benefits of each and their relevance to your own agenda you may decide that one is right for you. In some cases you may be required by an external agency to adopt the framework prescribed. You may also choose to go for an external award. Where you have freedom of choice be prepared to amend and adapt these frameworks so that they better suit your own purposes. You may even choose to write your own. In any case it will serve to pull together an otherwise disparate scattering of processes and projects into a coherent whole and provide the means by which the enormous range of possible approaches can be prioritized and integrated.

By this stage you will be in a position to formalize this activity and:

- *Draw up a quality policy statement*

This could include:

An introduction

for example:

— The importance of quality assurance
— The institution's commitment
— Relationship to overall strategy
— Existing systems and achievements
— Current weaknesses/improvements required
— Aims

The definition adopted

— Rationale
— Quality is defined as . . .

A strategic statement

For example:

> The College will adopt a TQM approach as the underpinning philosophy for quality improvement. We will seek accreditation as an Investor in People within the planning period seeing this as consistent with and a significant contribution to this process.
>
> We do not believe that quality can be inspected in but is best improved by the staff of the organization accepting responsibility for the continuous improvement of quality and provided with enough support and authority to make changes.
>
> Our approach will be to promote a series of quality improvement projects within the institution coordinated by the Vice Principal and the Quality Steering Group in line with the operational framework described below.

The operational framework to be used

— Examples of improvement projects under consideration
— Proposals for carrying the policy forward
— Management and resourcing issues
— The role of the steering group
— Targets

The publication of a document will allow for consultation and subsequent formal adoption by the institution. The document should receive wide circulation and formal adoption by significant committees such as:

— The Management Team
— The Academic Board
— The Governors

will normally be appropriate and will build momentum, support and credibility for what is proposed.

You will then be in a position to:

- *Identify a range of possible improvement projects for each element*

Taking each element of the framework in turn you should now be in a position to generate a comprehensive range of improvement projects which aligns itself with the mission, aims and strategy of the institution. Projects will not be hard to come by. The list should include consideration of:

— The review and evaluation of existing quality systems.
— Weaknesses and issues identified by external agencies, college management and the strategic planning process.

— Brainstorming within the steering group.
— Customer feedback.

If you have an effective team structure within the institution this could be the moment to share your ideas with them. Circulate the framework you propose as an agenda item.

— What do they think of it?
— What issues are important to them?
— Which projects would they favour or not favour under each of the headings?

All this will provide useful source material and prepare the ground for what is to follow. Do not be afraid of criticism. It is better to get people to articulate their concerns at an early stage while there is still time to alter course if necessary, sharpen up ideas as potential problems are unearthed, or at worst gauge the likely strength and views of the opposition!

This can be a very rewarding part of the exercise. If you are lucky considerable creativity will be unearthed, sometimes from unexpected quarters. Your own perspectives should begin to shift as you become better informed as a result of listening carefully to the feedback coming your way.

It is also easy to become confused, particularly if you harbour the ambition to see a consensus view emerge. Remember that consultation means 'to listen with an open mind'. It does not mean trying to do what you are told or seeking a consensus view which may only represent the lowest common denominator. The quality strategy should be strengthened by the debate but not overwhelmed by it.

An example

At this stage it might be useful to describe an example of how this approach might be used in practice. At Swindon, back in 1992, we used a heavily amended version of the Baldridge framework to get us started. The headings we set out were abbreviated as follows:

1   Satisfying customer needs
2   Quality of leadership
3   Management information
4   Quality assurance systems
5   Human resources
6   Planning

Since then much development work has been undertaken and there are a greater range of frameworks to be found. The EFQM award described earlier has openly built on the Baldridge approach. There are also a number of systems which have been specifically developed for education notably, SQMS, SQM and the Further Education Funding Council's *Assessing Achievement.*

The simplicity of the framework described above, however, does serve to emphasize a number of important points. The breadth of TQM becomes immediately apparent. It is not just about quality assurance systems as it can be argued is the case with ISO9000. Systems themselves are not enough. Neither is it only about human resource development and planning, which lie at the heart of Investors in People. TQM entails moving ahead on a wide variety of fronts drawing in, in due course, everyone and everything.

The framework can then be used to generate a series of questions which can in turn be used to suggest a series of improvement projects in each case.

1   Satisfying Customer Needs

Definition of Quality

- How does your definition of quality relate to customer needs?

Customer Satisfaction Surveys

- Have you devised a standard College Customer Survey Scheme for all lecturers, course and service teams and college managers? (see chapter 11).
- Have you devised and implemented a leavers form to monitor overall satisfaction with the course?
- Do you monitor levels for satisfaction with internal services? (see chapter 12).

FE Charter Review

- Have you reviewed the structure and operation of the College Charter?
- Does it meet the requirements of the Funding Council and the Department for Education and Employment (DfEE)?
- Does its contribute to quality improvement?
- Are staff and students aware of it?
- Have the commitments made in previous charters been honoured?
- Have you surveyed your students to determine whether they feel the commitments made have been honoured?
- Does your charter contain specific measurable, achievable commitments or a serious of broad commitments which might be better placed in the college prospectus?

Some examples:

Admissions, Guidance and Counselling
- We will acknowledge all enquiries and applications within five working days.

- You are entitled to an unbiased, confidential guidance interview with a qualified member of staff if required.
- We will communicate the results of the interview to you personally, in writing.
- We will provide individual information leaflets for all College-based courses.
- We will provide flexible start dates on many NVQ and GNVQ courses.
- You will have a personal tutor/mentor responsible for providing guidance and access to College support services.
- You will have the right to confidential, unbiased advice and careers guidance throughout your time as a student at the College.
- You are entitled to receive advice when applying for employment and further study.
- We will maintain a team of school liaison officers to provide advice on College courses in local schools.

Fees
- We operate a scheme for remitting fees in cases of hardship.
- We do not normally charge fees to students aged between 16 and 19 on full-time courses.
- We can advise on sources of funding and opportunities for gaining tax relief.
- We publish all costs associated with a course in advance.
- You will be entitled to a full refund of fees if we cancel your course.

Teaching and Learning
- You will be given an outline of the key dates for your programme.
- Your programme of learning will be planned with you to ensure that it meets your learning needs for personal development, employment or further study.
- Your achievements will be assessed both formally and informally during your period of study, and discussed with you.
- Your comments on your learning programme will be sought and taken into account in planning improvements.
- The College publishes a comprehensive set of standards for teaching and other College services. All staff will be encouraged to meet the high standards which have been set.
- You and the College will complete a Learning Agreement.
- You are entitled to make full use of the libraries and learning resources centres provided on the College's main sites.
- Open access computer facilities are provided on main college sites. You have the right to use them during the advertised opening hours (subject to availability).

Facilities for College-based Students

- You are entitled to participate in our programme of recreational, cultural and welfare activities.
- Where required we will help to find you somewhere to live and inspect recommended accommodation once a year.
- *You are entitled to make use of the following services:*

    * College Refectories
    * College Shops
    * Welfare and Counselling Services
    * Careers Guidance

- We provide a range of childcare facilities in support of students attending classes at the College's main sites.

Equal Opportunities

- We will provide study and enrolment opportunities in many centres throughout the area.
- We provide support for speakers of languages other than English.
- We provide wheelchair access to most specialist areas of the College and will move classes, whenever possible, in the event of difficulty.
- We will continue to promote a range of courses and other initiatives in support of the College's Equal Opportunities Policy, copies of which are available from Customer Services.

Employers and the Local Community

- We will maintain a team of employer liaison specialists led by the Business Development Manager.
- We will provide, for a fee, consultancy and customized programmes on request.
- We will undertake employer satisfaction surveys with specified companies on an annual basis.
- We can provide employee enrolment and information sessions on your premises if required.
- We will provide relevant information to employers and sponsors when required.

Complaints

We wish to provide a high quality service to all our customers. We recognize, however, that from time to time things will go wrong. In such circumstances we aim to put things right as quickly as possible and to learn from the experience as we seek to continuously improve the services we offer.

- If you have a complaint about any of the services we provide please contact the Customer Services Centres which will place your complaint in the hands of an appropriate College officer and keep you informed throughout the process.

Governance

The work of the College is overseen by the College Corporation, a group of local people who are responsible for supporting the College and oversight of its activities. A list of corporation members can be obtained from the Clerk to the Corporation at the address printed below.

The FEFC Inspectorate has completed a survey on college charters. Their main conclusions are discussed in chapter 10.

Colleges may be required to *publish* a charter, but they do have discretion over how much time and energy they put into them. This should be determined by the contribution these documents make to their quality assurance processes and the impact they have on their customers and the internal working of the college.

The Student Learning Agreement

- Have you devised and implemented a process by which students complete a Student Learning Agreement with their tutor which outlines the obligations expected on both sides?

2 Quality of Leadership

College Restructuring and Management Development

Where management is effective quality will improve.

- Is your management structure suitable for your current priorities?
- Do the people in that structure have the necessary skills?
- Does your management development programme develop the necessary skills and give proper emphasis to the management of quality and the operation of the college quality systems?

Team Development

- Have all College staff been assigned uniquely to teams?
- Are you looking at ways to empower and support them as they take responsibility for the courses/services they provide? (see chapter 6).

Delegated Budgets

- Is budget delegation being steadily cascaded through the system, moving decision making to its most appropriate level?

3 Management Information

Management Information Systems Review

- Is your MIS providing accurate timely reports to management and staff to support the range of performance indicators you require?
- Do you have an improvement strategy embracing staffing, hardware, software, management and systems?

Performance Indicators

- Have you drawn up and implemented a strategy for performance indicators? (see chapter 10).

4 Quality Assurance Systems

Team Review and Self-assessment

Sample material is provided in appendix 1 to support an annual system of team review and self-assessment. In this system:

- academic and service teams meet in June-September to reflect on outcomes and complete standard review and self-assessment documentation;
- documentation is presented to division/unit heads for action/consideration in the next College plan;
- action plans are produced covering the following:

    — Action to be taken by the team to improve the services provided
    — Action/support required from the College for consideration in the context of the College planning cycle
    — Staff development support required

New Course Approvals

Course approvals committees are widely used throughout further education to scrutinize new course proposals and often to measure the proposals against a set of pre-determined standards. An alternative and more flexible approach is described below:

- course 'ideas' are notified to the Director of Curriculum at the earliest opportunity;
- 'curriculum consultants', a group of trained and experienced College staff, are assigned to the development team to assist in development and monitoring of College quality standards;

- when a course is judged to have met the published course design standards (see appendix 1) approval is given by the consultant;
- 'approved' courses are notified to the Curriculum Director and the Academic Board. A course number is issued, signifying college approval to run the course.

Standards and Targets

A range of standards and targets may be adopted at various levels of the institution. Institutional targets can be linked to the achievement of college 'critical success factors'. The achievement of these targets internally can be reinforced through the faculty and directorate 'funding agreements' which link funding to the achievement of key performance targets (see chapter 10).

Detailing 'teaching standards' and 'course design standards' can be drawn up and adopted by the College (see chapter 10 and appendix 1). Staff teams are required to audit their performance against these standards using team review and self-assessment.

Directorate funding agreements can be made conditional on the achieving of agreed 'service standards' published in the College plan (see chapter 10).

Analysis of Student Achievements

A range of performance indicators including exam pass rates, completion rates and student progression will be compiled and published.

- Are there internal mechanisms for reviewing and evaluating the outcomes at institutional and team level?
- Are action plans drawn up?
- Are they implemented and reviewed?
- Are these issues reported to the Academic Board?

Policy and Procedures Documentation

Approved College policies and procedures should be documented and can be placed in official policies and procedures manuals.

The maintenance of the manuals should be the responsibility of a named manual coordinator. Copies of the manual can be widely distributed throughout the College and made the responsibility of official manual holders (see chapter 8).

A Central Complaints Logging System

Is there a central complaints logging and follow up system?

- Are customers aware of how they can complain?
- Is it straightforward for them to do so?

- Are complaints logged and assigned to an appropriate college officer for investigation?
- Is this service drawn to the attention of customers through the College Charter?

External Moderation and Inspection Arrangements

Schools and further education colleges differ significantly from HE institutions in that the majority of their provision is subject to external moderation and inspection arrangements by a number of agencies which include the following:

- Further Education Funding Council (FEFC)
- Office for Standards in Education (OFSTED)
- Higher Education Funding Council (England) (HEFCE)
- Validating bodies
- Examining boards
- Training and enterprise councils

The reports issued by these bodies can be a valuable source of information on the delivery of the course and the operation of certain quality systems.

- Do you have a system for reviewing these reports and picking up points requiring management action?

Quality Audit Team

- Does the institution have a 'Quality Audit Team' to audit the effectiveness and operation of key College quality systems? (see chapter 12).

5 Human Resources

Investors in People (IIP) Accreditation

The main focus of the Investor in People standard is in this area (see chapter 3).

Appraisal

- Do you have an effective system covering all staff, both teaching and support? (see chapter 9).
- Are part-time staff included?

A system for dealing with large numbers of part time staff is described in appendix 4.

Staff Development and Training, Planning, Policy and Budget

- Is the staff development plan and budget determined as part of the College planning cycle?
- Are there opportunities for staff to signal their development needs?
- Is there a strategic dimension with staff development used to promote corporate development and cultural change?

Internal Verification Procedures

- Do you have a comprehensive policy for internal verification and realistic targets for the training of internal verifiers? (see chapter 10).

Communications Improvement

- Do staff have sufficient information and understanding to take the decisions delegated to them?
- Do you have a strategy for communications improvement with associated action plan?

6 Planning

Planning and Reporting Cycle

- Do you maintain an open, visible planning and reporting process involving all staff supported by regular reviews?
- Is there sufficient attention given to the development of strategy?
- Are strengths and weaknesses and performance against objectives systematically evaluated?
- Do the results of this process inform the strategic planning cycle?

Having identified a range of possible initiatives the next key stage in the process must be to:

- Prioritize between possible improvement projects.

Your own intuition combined with an initial sifting at steering group may be sufficient at this point but those seeking a more structured approach may choose to predict their likely effect against some or all of the following.

— Organizational aims or critical success factors
— Identified organizational weaknesses

A matrix approach can help, for example:

Critical Success Factor/Aim	Proj 1	Proj 2	Proj 3	Proj 4
Improving Retention	X	X	/	
Better Student Support	X	/		/
Better Management Statistics	X		/	X
etc.				

x = significant effect
/ = some effect

In this example project 1 emerges a clear winner.

This approach can help you find your way through a wide range of competing claims, provided that the results are subjected to interpretation.

Other factors to be taken into account will include:

— the costs of the exercise and the scale of the benefits expected; and
— the need to build support for the programme and avoid unnecessary risks (particularly in the early stages).

Specifically:

— who will benefit and who will be most inconvenienced?
— will the results be results achievable?
— will the results be clear for all to see?

Once this exercise is complete it should be relatively easy to piece together and

• Publish a quality improvement plan

Each of the projects identified will need to be clarified, commissioned and monitored, probably using the steering group, to keep track of progress and amend the plan in the light of experience moving to the:

• Implementation phase

using the established principles of project management.

In parallel with implementation attention will need to be given to:

• Building support

The steering group should also be concerned to build support for the process using some or all of the following:

— consultation on quality policy, strategy and implementation;
— building, wherever possible on existing good practice and giving credit to it;
— selecting, in the early stages, projects which will readily bring conspicuous benefits to large numbers of people;
— systematically communicating your intentions and successes using existing media where possible and inventing new ones where these are inadequate (communications are dealt with in some detail in chapter 7);
— working closely with those charged with implementation (typically middle management or team leaders) to sharpen up proposals and ensure they are understood and promoted enthusiastically.

All this takes time. Do not overestimate what can be achieved and avoid the temptation to fix everything in the first year. By trying to do too much you may end up achieving nothing or even putting the clock back.

A possible approach to building and sustaining support, takes its cue from the leading quality guru Charles Deming. He argues that contrary to common practice most of the real issues which effect quality improvement are beyond the control of the workforce. They are, by and large, overwhelmingly management issues. Why not then start the process of quality improvement at management team level, effectively inviting management to become its own guinea pig?

Ineffective schemes can be eliminated before they are inflicted on the staff who may be further impressed by this outbreak of management by example.

Possible developments on this theme are outlined below.

A step-by-step approach

The term step-by step is used to describe an approach built on previous experience. Each layer builds on that which precedes it, but work on each layer continues indefinitely as the following diagram indicates:

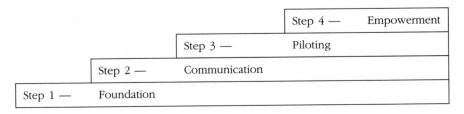

Each step is described in terms of the following:

Rationale

— The arguments in favour of the approach adopted in line with the preceding discussion.

Aims

— The aims of this particular operation phase.

Scope

— The parts of the organization directly involved.

Strategy

— Key elements of the strategy to be adopted in meeting these aims.

Core Activities and Project Options

— Instead of a standard system a range of project options is suggested for individual managers and teams to adopt in line with their assessment of the problems and priorities that they have identified.

These mechanisms will then be available within the 'step' in which they were developed and for use in all subsequent 'steps'.

These projects are to be developed in parallel with the operation of a small number of 'core activities' designed to move the organization step by step towards becoming an empowered team-based organization which fulfils the TQM criteria identified earlier.

The Steps in Detail

• Step 1 — Foundation

Rationale

Staff in the organization are likely to be suspicious of 'another management initiative' particularly in an area which can radically affect existing working practices and on an issue such as quality where many already hold strong professional views. Management must demonstrate its commitment by example, through concentrating early improvement efforts on the staff of the organization as 'internal customers' of the services provided by the management team before tackling the staff-external customer interface. During this phase a range of services which will support later stages of the operation will be built up and the necessary expertise and systems developed.

In addition, following Deming's assertion that the majority of quality problems are the province of management, by starting the process of quality improvement at management level the programme is immediately focused on areas where it is likely to have the greatest effect.

Aims

— To improve the effectiveness of the management team.
— To establish the needs of the organization customers.
— To plan and execute a quality improvement programme designed to provide the maximum benefit to the organization.
— To build support and credibility for further phases of the programme.

Scope

Initially only senior management will be directly involved in operations at this level.

Strategy

Identify potential areas of quality improvement under the control of senior management which are:

— Important to the organization
— Meet internal customer needs
— Readily achievable
— Demonstrable

Core Activities

Develop effective team working at management level using selection, team building and conflict management techniques as appropriate.

Survey the view of the team's internal and external customers as to the quality and scope of the services provided by the team.

Determine the organization's critical success factors.

Identify potential areas of quality improvement which address:

— critical success factors
— customer needs
and are readily achievable and demonstrable

Prioritize and select improvement projects according to the above criteria, deliver and evaluate.

Project Options

The selection of options will depend on the inclinations and abilities of the team in the context of their own circumstances. They may wish to draw on some or all of the following:

— team building techniques;
— conflict management techniques;
— use of TQM tools;
— formal clarification of team's customers;
— formal identification of services provided;
— definition of mission, aims and values.

- Step 2 — Communication

Rationale

Where there are successes they should be communicated in the broadest sense of the word. This is not simply advertising success but encouraging the flow of information, comment, debate and feedback to build support and participation in the enterprise in which the organization is involved.

Aims

To improve communications within the organization with a view of building support for the improvement process and achieving the ability to gauge the success of that enterprise.

Scope

The communication strategy will require the support of both senior and middle management. Team leaders will also be included in due course.

Strategy

Implement a communications improvement project.

Core Activities

— Consult on communication needs
— Draw up written policy on communication
— Determine strategy
— Develop and implement action plan
— Review

Project Options

- Information Systems Development Project

A review of the information systems requirements of the organization to include technical and support systems and management structures.

- Data Strategy Project

Determining the pattern of data, information and analysis required by staff teams, managers and external bodies in the planning and operation of the college. Building from this a comprehensive data and performance indicator strategy

- Step 3 — Piloting

Rationale

With the success of the quality improvement programme demonstrated by example and communicated to staff the next level moves on to tackle some of the more far reaching implications of TQM.

Aims

Volunteer teams are selected to pilot the introduction of self-directed work teams.

Scope

Senior and middle management with selected staff teams.

Strategy

To utilize the team development experience gained at management level at other levels of the organization and develop the concept of self-directed, continuously improving work teams, initially on a pilot basis.

Core Activities

'The team project' — a project designed to explore the meaning of the concept of the 'self-directed work team' providing a balance between:

(i)   responsibility — for the operation and continuous improvement of a defined set of services and courses;
(ii)   authority — to take the actions necessary to achieve this;
(iii) support — in terms of systems, training, resources etc.

Project Options

- The development of team appraisal
- Team review and self-assessment
- Professional support systems

— Finance and data systems development
— Teaching and service standards development: the development and operation of a system of team generated standards linked to college developed quality criteria
— College support team: establishing and training a team to support self-directed work teams in their operations and to assurance that College quality standards and procedures are being utilized.

- Step 4 — Empowerment

Rationale

Following on from the experience gained in the pilot phase the self-directed work teams concept is extended to the whole organization.

Aims

To create an empowered organization.

Scope

The whole College.

Strategy

Extending the team project, revised in the light of experience, to the whole organization.

Chapter 6

Management and Staff

Management

As has been discussed earlier both theory and practice suggest that the role of senior management in the process of quality management will determine the fate of the whole process. The Chief Executive's commitment must be unquestioned and outspoken. There are too many hard things to do and too many opportunities to do something else over too long a timescale for quality improvement programmes to survive the benign neglect of the institution's head. The strategy and its implementation must be strongly identified in the minds of the staff with a senior figure who has linked his/her reputation to the course laid out.

As discussed in the last chapter middle management also has a crucial role to play as they will be responsible for carrying and interpreting messages on a day-to-day basis and influencing the choices that staff must make as to how they use their time. Their views on what they can and wish to achieve should be sought and understood.

As discussed in the last chapter middle management also has a crucial role to play as they will be responsible for carrying and interpreting messages on a day-to-day basis and influencing the choices that staff must make as to how they use their time. Their views on what they can and wish to achieve should be sought and understood.

Staff Teams

If your quality strategy, as suggested earlier, aims to transfer ownership and responsibility for quality improvement to the staff of the organization, the role of the staff team in this process cannot be underestimated. The importance of team work in any organization is well documented. There are few educational organizations which do not use the term or recognize the existence of teams within their organizational structure. From the perspective of quality improvement teams have the potential to provide:

- a forum for the review, development and continuous improvement of a service or curriculum area;

- a mechanism for mutual support, communication and peer involvement;
- a stable structure to whom authority and accountability for operations can be delegated;
- a mechanism to move debate and decision making to its optimum point in the organization;
- a group which will self-regulate, self-assess and self-motivate.

Teams are, of course, well established throughout education. From the subject 'teams' in 'A' level and GCSE departments through to the more complex course teams, strongly promoted by organizations such as the Business and Technology Education Council (BTEC), to support the more integrated approach to course delivery which developed during the 1980s.

In most circumstances the course team is not a sufficiently stable structure to deliver the agenda outlined above. Staff will typically belong to a number of course teams simultaneously and will move from one to another on an annual basis. In many cases they will not have the opportunity to develop a strong sense of ownership for the development of the team, or accept accountability for its success or failure.

For these reasons, individuals should not normally belong to more than one 'base team' although they may provide a service to other teams. Everyone in the organization is assigned to one unique base team and stays with it and works within it long enough to feel implicated in its successes and failures.

If a team such as this were to become fully 'self-directing' they would pick up a whole range of new responsibilities and would need the power and authority to match these. The final vision of this process could be summarized as a Self-directing Work Team.

Self-directed Work Teams

Definition

A highly trained group, normally six-twelve people, fully responsible for the delivery of a well-defined segment of a product or service.

Teams might be expected to take on a range of responsibilities and powers which could include: to act at all times within College guidelines, policies and procedures and attend appropriate training in this regard.

Nature of Product/Service

- To negotiate a plan and contract to deliver all or part of (a range of) a product service(s) in line with existing/future customer expectations.
- To develop new services in a defined area for identified customers.
- To develop the service in detail.

- To set criteria for selection of students.
- To operate the product/service within corporate guidelines/policies.
- To provide services to other teams.
- To contract with the College to deliver all/part of a course or service.
- To decline such contracts not allowed for in the team plan.
- To meet and be accountable for targets related to:

      (i)   quality
      (ii)   volume/enrolments
      (iii) financial procedures
      (iv) production of reports
      (v)   contractual standards

- To control class sizes/course hours/course calendar.
- To determine professional standards.

Physical Resources

- To ensure the maintenance and security of such physical resources as are allocated to the team.
- To purchase resources within the limits of available funds.
- To make unused resources including accommodation available to other teams as required.
- To lease/let resources to outside customers.
- To plan investment in equipment, stationery and materials.
- To determine the use of accommodation allocated to the team.
- To ensure the maintenance and development of accommodation allocated.
- Subject to purchasing guidelines to choose suppliers.

Financial

- To be given a one-line budget and the power to operate subject to Financial Regulations.
- To manage a one-line delegated budget to include:

      (i)   full and part-time staff (teaching and support)
      (ii)   apparatus and equipment
      (iii) materials

- Subject to Scheme of Delegation, to vire between expenditure heads.
- To accept risk.
- To meet financial targets.

Human Resources

- To deploy human resources effectively.
- To control membership of the team.
- Operate within personnel policies and procedures and conditions of service.
- To control team administration, agendas, calendars, etc.
- To control appointment and dismissal (within regulations).
- To abide by guidelines of promotion, appointment, induction, etc.
- To determine rewards within existing College mechanisms.
- To undertake/be involved in appraisal.
- To determine timetables/work schedules.
- To take part in team review and self-assessment and produce reports.
- To support/develop staff and produce a staff development plan.
- To choose/develop specialisms within the team.

Marketing (Internal/External)

- To promote all the products/services provided by the team to internal/external customers.
- To work with the marketing staff to promote team courses/services as appropriate.

Information

- To provide information, data and reports on the activities of the team as required.
- To have access to College information systems.
- To maintain databases relevant to the activities of the team.

Very few institutions would want or be able to move directly to implement something along the lines described above. In the short term more modest goals would allow time for development and reflection on the likely long-term benefits to the organization. A step-by-step approach could be to:

- *Decide on the team structure to be adopted*

Different areas of the institution will have different perspectives as to what their teams should be. Within the principle of each staff member belonging to only one team the optimum division can normally be left to local debate and decision. The key must be to find a natural focus around which the group can coalesce.

For example, this could be a subject such as 'mathematics' or a whole programme area. It could be based on a market segment such as 'provision for the unemployed' or a service such as 'personnel' or 'finance'. This will save a lot of team development time further down the track if the members of the team already recognize the affinity that pre-exists between them. The question of leadership may also be left open at this stage. Some teams will already have a leader in post, whereas in others there is a natural candidate. Things are more tricky where none is available or the team itself does not want a leader. For the time being a communications 'link' may be sufficient and more controversial aspects can be left until the operations of the team are more firmly embedded.

- *Publicize the team structure and maintain it*

The team structure and membership will be in a constant state of flux as staff move in and out of the organization and priorities change. Your hard won team structure will soon decay unless a system is put in place to track and record the changes. There are many mechanisms for this. One I have used with some success involved publishing the team structure as a classified section in the College phone directory. This proved to be a useful document in itself. It also meant the directory was automatically updated on at least an annual basis and errors more likely to attract comment.

- *Survey attitudes to team development*

In determining how fast and far it is prudent to go in the development of teams a survey of staff attitudes can provide useful source material.

The survey could enquire whether existing teams:

- have a clear statement of team responsibilities;
- meet regularly as a team;
- share tasks;
- share decision-making;
- share resources;
- give and receive feedback;
- contribute to planning;
- undertake regular self-assessment;
- operate an equipment and materials budget;
- operate a fully delegated 'one line' budget (including staffing);
- draw up their own work schedules and holidays;
- determine the division of staff responsibilities;
- achieve good communications within the team;
- achieve good communications with other teams;
- have clear plans for quality improvement;
- set their own standards and targets;
- initiate innovation and development;

- understand clearly the standards they must reach;
- are involved in staff appointments;
- have adequate access to clerical support;
- have adequate access to PCs with appropriate software;
- have adequate access to the College computer network;
- regularly hold/attend team briefing sessions.

Depending on the results of this exercise you should be in a position to:

- *Set stage 1 targets*

Teams are likely to be in a different state of development across the institution. The aim of stage 1 would be to bring all teams up to an achievable minimum standard of team development.
Modest short-term targets could include:
- a delegated small equipment and materials budget;
- a statement of income earned against total expenditure;
- team devised timetables and work schedules;
- involvement in all appointments to the team;
- maintaining a data base of courses/services operated by the team;
- maintaining a database of students/customers linked to courses/services provided by the team;
- negotiating/achieving targets for:

    (i) enrolments/service volume
    (ii) retention/achievement
    (iii) appraisal
    (iv) customer satisfaction/the achievement of service standards

- maintaining a clear team structure/membership list;
- maintaining a statement of the divisions of responsibilities within the team;
- a schedule of appraisals;
- a plan of curriculum/service development;
- a cycle of customer satisfaction surveys and responses;
- a record of the self-assessment process;
- evidence for quality audit indicators;
- completing team review and self-assessment.

As part of this process it will be necessary to:

- *Identify support and training*

The agenda outlined above implies that the following support would need to be provided:

- training in team operations and development;
- training in team leadership skills;
- support from a management mentor;
- time for meetings according to a pre-published calendar;
- access to administrative support;
- access to networked PCs;
- negotiated standards, plans and targets;
- information on budgets and expenditure.

- *Implications for management*

As teams become more confident and better able to take decisions for themselves the role of management begins to change. Characteristically the role becomes more of support and mentor rather than line manager. A crucial point arrives when the line management link is broken and the former line manager is no longer accountable for the performance of the team. They continue to have an extensive role in supporting teams in their new found freedoms although the numbers involved in this activity may change as managers are redeployed into other areas, or reduced in numbers, hopefully through 'natural wastage'. The need for ongoing support should ensure that the process is a gradual one with few if any unexpected causalities along the way.

- *The next steps*

It is for the institution to decide how far and how fast it wishes to move towards the team 'vision' described earlier. Progress will depend on the outcome of the intermediate stages outlined above.

The organization will be concerned to ensure that the division of the organization into teams does not worsen any instances of territorialism which may characterize existing arrangements. Teams are, however, likely to sit very well within the academic environment where traditions of individual independence have sat uncomfortably within the new order of managerial control and corporatism.

The notion of independent peer groups gaining the maximum of operational autonomy, but now within an overall strategic framework at institutional level, may in the long run prove more motivating and satisfying than current arrangement dictate.

Achieving Cultural Change

'Changing the culture' is widely held up as an essential prerequisite if educational institutions are to survive and prosper in the new climate. There is, however, less unanimity on what features of the existing culture must change and what they should change to.

We are, however, undeniably beset by change and 'cursed to lived in interesting times'. Further education must compete and in order to compete it must develop a more market-led perspective with greater focus on the needs of the individual customer. It must move with flexibility and speed to capitalize on market opportunities as and when they become apparent. As if this were not enough it must become more financially efficient and demonstrate that it has improved quality, particularly the quality of its outcomes. And in all this it must be more and more accountable.

In broad terms there were two cultures operating within pre-incorporated colleges. The dominant academic culture, a professional tendency with individuals owing their primary allegiance to their subject specialism and the students currently within their care. Quality (if the word was ever used) was an individual and often private responsibility. The dominant culture coexisted, often uneasily, with the bureaucratic culture of the administration.

Since incorporation the main thrust of cultural change can be seen in the following areas.

- *Corporatism*

The dominant academic culture has been challenged by the emergence of the 'corporation' seeking the allegiance of all staff to the institution, its missions aims and strategic goals.

- *Customer focus*

In the development of new provision the balance is shifting from 'what else can we do?' to 'what else do they want?' Powerful marketing directorates have been developed to give additional impetus to this development. Inevitably academic staff feel their traditional dominance in this area is threatened.

- *Financial awareness*

The continuing search for financial efficiency at College level and funding mechanisms which follow the student are gradually forcing the need for financial awareness down through the system.

- *Accountability*

We are no longer to be left to look after quality as a professional responsibility. We must measure, set targets, publish and demonstrate improvement.

Achieving the Change

The culture of any institution is changing all the time as it reacts organically to pressures in its internal and external environment. The question for the organization and its management is whether or not they wish to attempt to control this change and to unify its effects across the organization.

If the answer to this question is yes, then it must:

- clarify what elements of the existing culture it will seek to change;
- discuss its aims widely throughout the organization;
- seek to determine what prevents the change from taking place or renders it ineffective;
- avoid actions/messages which reinforce the status quo;
- develop and implement mechanisms which promote the desired changes.

The change agenda outlined above will be influenced by the following:

- *Systems*

    (i)   Planning systems which conspicuously draw on the ideas of all staff and combine them within a strategic perspective to ensure that the views of staff are influential in drawing together the strategy and development of the institution.
    (ii) Resourcing systems which reward enterprise and provide teams with a proportion of what they earn.
    (iii) Customer surveys which provide staff with feedback from students and other internal and external customers.
    (iv) Reward systems which reward good practice which furthers the objectives of the institution.
    (v)   'One line' systems which treat all staff so far as possible equally.

- *Communications*

    (i)   A strategic approach to communications which determines what, when and how key messages are to be communicated to those concerned.
    (ii) IS/IT systems, which provide the information staff need to support informed and rational decision-making.

- *Training*

    (i)   Structured and proactive training programmes that reinforce the requirement for cultural change and develop the skills necessary to perform effectively in the new environment.
    (ii) An appraisal system which addresses the role each individual has in achieving institutional objectives and identify the support necessary to achieve this.

- *Delegation*

    (i)   Full financial delegation to team level to ensure an element of financial understanding and risk is felt at all levels.

    (ii)   Team development to encourage independence and accountability to staff team level.

    (iii)   Empowerment of teams to provide for better decision making at the most relevant point in the organization.

- *Audit*

Systematic checking for evidence of systems being operated and standards achieved.

Budgetary Delegation

Budgetary delegation provides one of the most powerful mechanisms for the empowerment of teams. The benefits the organization can expect from internal delegation will include:

- *Ease of administration*

The need to refer even the most minor items of expenditure for approval by relatively highly placed managers introduces delay and often frustration. The costs in mangement and administrative time can also be considerable and must eventually find their way on to the bottom line when staffing levels are up for review. Just as damaging is the atmosphere of mistrust that it engenders. There is no great skill in managing a simple cash budget. We all do it in our everyday lives so why not at work?

- *Flexibility*

While the request for authorization sits around in someone's in-tray a rival organization, able to move more flexibly, may have moved and gained a competitive advantage. Imagine the cumulative effect of more rapid decision making throughout the whole organization. Moreover the effect of a bureaucratic, controlled environment will be to discourage innovation and flexibility.

- *Financial efficiency*

If decision-making is moved down to the level where the problem is best understood then the quality of decision taken must improve. In an undelegated environment it is logical for staff to press for additional resources in all areas. In some cases they will be successful, in others they will not. Each case will be taken separately and the decision will depend on the prevailing circumstances at the time and the views of those who take the decision.

In a previous college, as head of department I always felt that we were overstaffed with science technicians. Although comparisons with other institutions tended to support this view there were (and there always are) special circumstances. The staff were unanimous that the existing complement was vital to enable them to continue their work. Why should they think anything else? They had nothing to gain and much to lose. Enter the delegated budget. Now the problem posed was altogether different. If the technician complement was reduced then the resources would be made available to them in some other way. They had to choose whether they were using the resources allocated to them in the most effective way. When the opportunity arose, they chose to reduce the technician staff and put the resources into equipment and refurbishment.

Another group of lecturers decided to combine classes which could be effected in large lecture groups and use the resources freed up to provide individual tutorials while preparing project work. Not only did this decision require a detailed knowledge of the course and how it was and could be taught but it also depended on having a number of reliable part-time staff, in whom they had confidence, available to increase the staffing at the appropriate time of the year.

In each case delegation of decision-making had resulted in the available resources being deployed more efficiently.

- *Quality improvement*

I have argued that quality in education is best improved by encouraging staff to take responsibility for it and providing them with sufficient authority and support necessary to do so. The importance of teams has also been considered. Financial delegation is evidently an important part of that process with its role in promoting quality improvement through better decision-making, more effective use of resources and the encouragement of team work.

Delegation opens up a new professional role for teachers in a world where pressure on resources is an established and permanent reality. We ask them to make choices and to provide the best possible quality at the price that society is prepared to pay.

Supporting Delegation

Before making any moves towards a delegation strategy to support it should be in place. Delegation itself is probably best undertaken as a gradual process leaving time for each step to be evaluated and any problems eliminated before more radical measures are taken. The component parts of any support strategy should include:

- *Training*

> (i) In team work and team leadership.
> (ii) In budgeting and budgetary control.
> (iii) In the use of basic IT packages.

- *Information*

Are your communication systems sufficiently open and comprehensive to support decision-making at lower levels of the organization?

- *Support*

> (i) Will access to a PC and the computer network be required?
> (ii) Is administrative/secretarial support possible and appropriate?
> (iii) Are office facilities adequate?

- *Systems*

> (i) Are your information systems, particularly your financial systems capable of supporting delegation to the level proposed?
> (ii) Are policies and procedures well documented and readily accessible to those who will need to refer to them?

- *Audit and monitoring*

> (i) Are your audit and monitoring systems adequate to pick up irregularities or give reasonable warning of budgetary overspend?
> (ii) Do procedures no longer requiring authorization in advance still maintain a satisfactory audit trail?

- *Mentoring*

Are experienced managers available to support and help, particularly in the early phases?

Chapter 7

Communications

Improving communications should be high on the agenda of any quality improvement programme. Good communications are essential to:

- provide the information staff require to support decision-making in a delegated environment;
- support the development of a corporate culture and minimize the differences of view between management and staff;
- ensure the ideas and perspectives of staff are drawn into the development and direction of the institution;
- provide opportunities for the vision aims and objectives of the institution to be shared.

Communications, of course, can be both formal and informal. Managers will be concerned to communicate their views to staff but the provision of opportunities for staff to communicate with management should not be neglected. Of equal importance are the day-to-day communications between individuals, groups and teams. The management maxim, 'communicate, communicate, communicate' should be adopted by all.

The rule

- consider   who will be affected
- consult   with those involved
- communicate   any decisions taken

should be universally applied.

It may be, particularly in smaller organizations, that informal communications are sufficient. In a typical, multisite FE college, however, a more structured approach will be worth the investment.

In drawing up and implementing a strategy on communications consult with staff to draw out areas of common concern and ideas for overcoming them. Formulate a communications strategy and associated action plan followed by a number of prioritized communications improvement projects, introduced as time and resources permit.

- *Consultation*

There are of course many ways of achieving this. One approach involves using a simple unstructured questionnaire, distributed to all staff which asked the question: list up to three ways in which improvements in college communications could help you do your job more effectively?

This approach will provide plenty of ideas as to what can be done, in addition to those you may have thought up for yourself. Such a survey will give you a feel for the concerns and priorities of staff, which could help inform the drawing up of the communications strategy. Finally, as you move to implement the strategy, you will be able to show that many of the actions you have taken have been supported by the staff.

A Strategy for Employee Communications — An Example

Aim

To enable members of the College to build and share a vision of where the College is going through the creation of an open structure for the exchange of information, ideas and beliefs.

Objectives

A list of objectives might include some of the following:

1 To create clear lines of communication covering all staff.
2 To communicate the goals of the organization to staff.
3 To create clear mechanisms for the involvement of all members of the College in the operation and the strategic development of the organization.
4 To increase the visibility and approachability of management.
5 To provide increased opportunities for informal communication.
6 To reduce duplication, information overload and bureaucracy.
7 To give greater emphasis to:

  (i) verbal communication;
  (ii) communication from staff to management;
  (iii) communication to and from part time staff;
  (iv) communication between internal customers and the providers of services.

8 To reduce the number of steps in the communication process.
9 To identify communication as a designated management team responsibility.

10 To encourage good communication practice between all members of the College and the use of plain English.

Having decided and prioritized your objectives consider for each in turn what practical actions can be taken to achieve each of them. What follows is intended as a list of ideas to assist in this process.

- *Clarify line management/communication links*

For every member of the organization:

(i)   is communicating with them someone's responsibility?
(ii)   is it in their job specification?
(iii) do they understand the importance of that responsibility?

If your organization is based on teams is it clear which team each individual member of staff belongs to? If they work with several teams is it clear which is their base team (or 'home team') for communication purposes. In many cases it will be necessary to undertake a team mapping exercise and publish the results. You will also need a mechanism for updating the constant staff movements, changes and team restructuring.

If you have teams how will communication work within the team and beyond it? Is this part of the role of the team leader or a separate designated responsibility within the team?

Special consideration is needed here for part-time staff. They can be responsible for a significant proportion of your teaching and therefore a significant proportion of your quality but they are harder to communicate with and less likely to be familiar with the corporate culture. When part-time or temporary staff are taken on is it made clear to them and to the administration who is to be their communication link? Do your systems allow for their details to be entered on the staff database?

- *Turn the phone book into a classified team directory*

The internal phone directory can be an invaluable aid to communications. It should include

(i)   familiar names;
(ii)   office room numbers;
(iii) team membership.

With today's database technology, however, it is possible to go one step further and in addition to the usual alphabetical listing, publish a classified section, classified by team membership. The annual updating of your phone list will also provide a mechanism for keeping your team listings up to date.

- *Introduce weekly team briefings*

One of the problems you run into when you try and improve communications is that it is difficult to do so on any scale without increasing the amount of paper in circulation and staff already have so much to read that they will not welcome any more, no matter how worthy its intentions. Weekly team briefing sessions supported by briefing notes can provide at least part of the answer.

Briefing notes are produced once a week, usually just after a management team meeting, which normally generates some items of interest. They are distributed to team leaders who use them as part of a regularly scheduled team meeting or a brief additional meeting called for that purpose, the former being more likely to be effective in the long-term.

Team briefings offer a number of advantages.

(i) The briefing is verbal, no extra paperwork to read.

(ii) They provide an opportunity for discussion or identify a need for further clarification.

(iii) They can provide a mechanism for feedback to management via line management relationships or a feedback sheet.

(iv) They allow for rapid consultation between the management team and staff. As a response can be made within the week, decisions can be delayed until staff views have been determined.

(v) They strengthen both corporate and team identify.

- *Involve staff in the planning cycle*

Educational institutions are unique in the intellectual capacity and range of specialisms represented by their staff. Teaching staff, in particular, have seen much of their independence diminished as pressure for accountability and corporatism increase. One of the aims of the communication process must be to draw on the intellectual capacity of the organization and build ownership amongst the staff for the planning process and the overall strategic direction of the organization. One of the most important mechanisms I propose in this respect is the operation of an integrated planning, budgeting and quality system based on team review and self-assessment. This proposal is described in more detail in chapter 12.

- *Face to face with the boss*

The principal or headteacher is more than a Chief Executive. They maintain their traditional role as a figurehead for the institution and are expected to display a sense of pastoral responsibility for both staff and students. It is important for the boss to be out and about and for staff to have the opportunity to talk with him or her and debate the issues of the day. Small group settings, no more than twenty people, with no pre-determined agenda can be an effective and valuable use of time. Smaller groups allow for a genuine exchange of information and views and over time help considerably in bringing the organization together. Seeing all the staff in such a setting over an annual cycle should prove possible in all but the largest colleges.

This approach can be extended to other managers in the organization to considerable effect.

Other opportunities for direct face to face communication can come from

(i)   involvement in staff training/induction;
(ii)   walkabouts;
(iii) being available in common rooms etc.

- *Cascade presentations*

This technique is used in some large commercial organizations to communicate the contents of key documents, such as the corporate plan or annual report, to staff. Translated into the educational world it can also be used to get feedback on draft proposals before they are implemented or simply to sample opinion within the organization.

1   A draft presentation is prepared, with supporting documentation, transparencies, etc.
2   The presentation is made to middle managers in a small group session (normally up to twenty). The message and style of the presentation are then discussed openly with those present.
3   In the light of the comments made the presentation is modified along the lines suggested and the revised materials distributed to those who attended the first presentation.
4   Each manager then makes the presentation to his/her team. Comments made in the discussion which follows are fed back.

There are evident advantages to this technique.

(i)   It allows for the views of middle managers to be built into the proposal and the presentation, increasing both ownership and commitment.
(ii)   It allows for discussion of the issues raised, ensuring more effective communication than a conventional presentation.
(iii) It provides an immediate mechanism for feedback.

- *Management restructuring*

Are so many layers of management really necessary? As empowered teams take over more responsibilities previously exercised by management it becomes inevitable that fewer management positions will be necessary. Delayering, as the management jargon goes, is rife in industry and not unknown in education. The gain for communication comes in reducing the number of steps in the communication process and reduction in the distance between senior management and staff.

- *Upgrade the newsletter*

There is plenty of advice about on how to present and structure the company newsletter. The approach in education may need to be rather different from that employed by commercial organizations in recognition of the different culture and traditions we have.

Ask yourself the following:

- Do senior managers write all or most of the articles?

If so it will probably be seen as a propaganda tool and may not be widely read. Try commissioning articles on points of interest from other members of staff, invite others to contribute by a published deadline.

- Is the content too dry or one sided?

Staff will be interested in good news about the organization, but they will also have concerns which they will expect to see answered. What will this year's deficit mean for them? Are you really planning to sell off the car park for a shopping mall? Would you believe a newspaper that only peddled good news? People like to read about people. Comings and goings, births, marriages and even deaths.

- Does it look too smart or too 'tatty'?

Too tatty and it will not be credible but if it attempts to emulate the glossy publications produced by major multinationals it will distance itself from its audience. After all the money has to come from somewhere.

- *Use technology*

Technological development is providing a whole range of new options to support improvements in communication. The use of EMail is already having an effect in many colleges. It is easier and faster than sending a memo and it encourages a swift response. You don't need to call back when the person you want to reach is out of the office. EMail can also allow for better targeting of messages to groups of users throughout the system.

Other areas where technology is beginning to make an impact include:

(i)   voice mail;
(ii)   internal mobile phone systems;

(iii)   internal bulletin board;
(iv)   computer home links.

Research has shown that staff perceptions of their main source of information directly correlates with job satisfaction. In general staff who feel they get most information directly from their line manager are the most content. In descending order come staff briefings, the company newsletter, noticeboards, the local press and the unions.

Suggesting ways in which communication can be improved is easy enough. If only there was enough time to do everything. The trick of course comes in deciding which courses of action are likely to have the greatest effect. To help you through this process:

(i)   prioritize your objectives;
(ii)   decide which objectives each project will contribute to.

Those with a dedicated analytical approach may find the matrix approach described earlier to be helpful.

To finish this section a few more ideas.

- Set up a system for distributing material to designated noticeboards.
- Survey the views of staff as 'customers' of the services provided by the management team.
- Publish an annual calendar/wall planner including dates of college meetings, planning deadlines, term dates etc.
- Publish an 'executive summary of the College plan and distribute it to all staff. Use design to emphasize the messages you are trying to communicate rather than just edit down the words of the original.
- Rota staff common room visits into your diary to make time for that all important informal communication.

Chapter 8

Processes and Procedures

Following incorporation, the trend in further education colleges had been to reduce the proportion of expenditure spent on academics while increasing the proportion of administrative and support staff. To some extent this was unavoidable. Colleges needed to take on staff to do jobs, such as personnel and finance, which were previously undertaken by the local authorities. There was also, however, the view that relatively highly paid academics were undertaking a range of tasks which could be performed more cost effectively by other staff. 'Horses for courses' became an important principle in achieving greater financial efficiency.

In effect this principle is based on the belief that by dividing a process up into its component parts and between a number of discrete functions, individuals performing those functions can achieve a high degree of competence in their specialist area and in many cases those services can be obtained more cheaply than might otherwise have been the case. This is often true. There is, however, a powerful counter argument.

The problem with specialization is that different parts of each process have to be handed from one individual to another. There are inevitable problems with coordination, no-one has an overview of the whole process and 'handover' time, that is the elapsed time between the job being put down by one individual and picked up again by another introduces delay, inflexibility and inefficiency. Moreover, it is argued, proper training, combined with the back-up of modern information systems technology can extend an individual's competence over a far wider range of skills than would have been the case in the past.

The proponents of 'business process engineering' go on to suggest that a fresh look at our processes might lead to a complete redesign, eliminating unnecessary hand-ons, doing away with superfluous checks and sometimes even trusting the customer to do some of the work for us.

Perhaps one-day information systems will be so advanced and widely distributed as to enable academic staff to enrol students, collect fees by electronic transfer, and enter students for examinations without having to leave the classroom.

Under local authority control many of the systems which have been passed to us through incorporation or local management arrangements were designed to make fraud impossible. Often the real cost of these systems was far more than the cost of any fraud was ever likely to be. The emphasis is now changing in favour of more efficient systems while ensuring that there is an audit trail which would enable fraud to be traced if and when it should occur.

Some examples:

(i) A College operated an internal transfer system between internal budget holders which required the signatures of both parties. Unfortunately debtors often proved to be extremely reluctant to sign the transfer forms sometimes referring to minor discrepancies which bounced back and forth, through the College's overstretched Finance Department. The effect produced deteriorating relationships between budget holders and distorted the management accounts. The process was 'reengineered'. Once a price has been agreed a direct debit system operates with an immediate cash transfer effected by the Finance Department. In rare cases where disputes arise there is provision for pendulum arbitration, the so-called star chamber, which rules in favour of one party or the other.

(ii) The College is involved in a partnership nursery and has the right to take up a set number of places. If it does not fill up these places it leases them on to other partners who require the space. Previously the nursery invoiced the College for all its places and the College then invoiced any other partners it had leased places to. In fact this was quite a complex process as the number of places leased was never the same from one month to the next. The nursery now deals direct with each partner for the exact number of places they occupy. No more work for them and significantly less for the partners.

The link with quality is I hope becoming clear. If processes are simpler and more efficient then the benefits to the customer, both internal and external, will soon be evident to all concerned. Speed of response and reliability of service are bound to improve. If the process can also be completed more cheaply then that should free up scarce resources to be deployed elsewhere.

This approach is an illustration of Deming's assertion that the majority of quality improvement issues are management problems. Exhorting the staff operating in these areas may result in a marginal improvement but the quantum leap which may result from a reengineered process will normally require management action.

As information systems develop, tasks which were previously the responsibility of employees are increasingly being left to the customer. Telephone and computer banking has removed the bank clerk from the chain, some supermarkets are training customers to 'check out' their own goods on a portable scanner as they go round the store (with the occasional spot check to encourage customer honesty) and when did a pump attendant last fill your petrol tank for you?

In colleges we may wish to take this approach one step further. Our goal should be not only to encourage customers to take on some tasks we might previously have done for them but, wherever possible, to use this experience to promote learning.

In a world where we are subject to the twin pressures of improving quality and reducing costs the fundamental problem for educational managers can be expressed as:

How do we create more learning with less teaching?

Part of the answer lies in making the individual more responsible for his/her own learning and involving them more in the learning process.

There are in effect already many examples of what could be termed 'learning process reengineering' developing throughout education. The use of radical new approaches to learning which place more emphasis on the role of the student can be clearly seen in:

- resource-based learning;
- work-based learning;
- accreditation of prior learning;
- computer-based learning and information systems.

The role of the teacher is itself changing as they become more managers of learning, responsible for the structure and oversight of the whole learning process with less significance placed on activities within the classroom itself.

The involvement of students in delivering College processes is not to be restricted only to teaching and learning. As technology advances it will become possible to involve them in a greater range of administrative activities. There are already examples of student completing the enrolment process themselves, sometimes remotely over the Internet, guided only by the information provided over the computer screen. Students will increasingly maintain their own performance and attendance records, enter examinations for themselves and in some cases mark their own tests. In some cases such activity may be used to develop and reinforce learning implying a blurring of the distinction between the academic and administrative functions of the organization.

Such developments will require:

- a radical reappraisal of the organization's processes;
- trusting that most individuals will be honest most of the time;
- support from information systems;
- robust audit systems to enable the occasional transgressor to be brought to book.

A Procedures Manual System

The best, most efficient, processes in the world will not be of much help if those who are required to operate them fail to do so. They will certainly fail to do so if they are not aware of them and do not understand them. In an empowered, highly delegated organization an increasing range of procedures will need to be understood and operated by a growing number of people.

All but the smaller educational institutions will ultimately benefit from setting up and maintaining a system of manuals containing up to date information on all significant policies and procedures.

A procedures manual system will:

- provide a clear set of rules for the operation of the institution;
- act as an aid to communication;
- support delegation;
- provide mechanisms for the official recognition of College policy;
- eliminate duplication or potential contradiction;
- reinforce corporate behaviour;
- support management and staff in their operational duties;
- provide a mechanism for reviewing and updating College policy;
- provide a framework for audit.

In some cases the provision of a well documented set of procedures will be seen as of sufficient importance to justify the additional effort required to achieve external accreditation, ISO 9000 series being the obvious candidate. In such circumstances institutions will wish to follow the rules set down by the standard and the accreditation body.

Those who are driven by other priorities and wish to set their own development agenda may find the following description useful.

A Manual System Described

A policies and procedures manual system can build to become a comprehensive set of reference materials on all the main policies and procedures operated within the institution. By adopting a loose leaf binder format updates, revisions and additions can be easily accommodated allowing the system to live and grow as organizational requirements change.

Normally a number of separate manuals will be required, for example:

- general administration;
- information systems;
- health and safety;
- personnel;
- finance;
- student administration;
- planning;

- quality;
- curriculum;
- corporation;
- marketing.

Each of the above should have an individual coordinator responsible for circulating revisions and additions to all the manual holders. They should also make sure that the content of their manual is up-to-date and meets the needs of the organization. It obviously makes sense for the coordinator to be the responsible officer in each particular area, for example the Health and Safety Officer, Personnel Manager etc.

Each manual should contain:

- an index of policies/procedures with issue revision date;
- a list of coordinators;
- a list of manual holders and locations.

For each individual policy or procedure the following should be identified, preferably using a common header sheet to emphasis a consistent approach.

- Manual name
- Section

  It will sometimes be useful to split a manual up into a number of different sections.

- Title
- Issue status

  e.g. — Guideline (circulated by the coordinator)
  — Draft (for consultation)
  — Policy (approved by management team)
  — Corporation (adopted by the corporation)

- Date of issue
- Document number

  Essential for the updating process

- Date of next revision

  By entering the revision date of each policy on a database the system administrator can contact each coordinator in advance of a policy going out of date to ensure that the policy is revised in time. It also enables 'progress chasing' when a response is not forthcoming. This facility also provides a valuable mechanisms for ensuring policies are checked from time to time to see if they are still valid or necessary. Timescales should be neither too ambitious or over long. Three years seems to be an appropriate norm, but shorter times will be necessary in some cases, for example, particular procedures following the annual academic cycle, or

important new procedures requiring a early
revisit.

- Manual Coordinator   As described above
- Maintainer   The coordinator, while remaining responsible
for the manual as a whole, may seek to sub-
contract individual policies to other individuals
to enable workload to be shared or to draw on
their expertise.
- Arrangements for review   As each policy is different the procedure for
reviewing it will vary. In some cases it will be
sufficient for the coordinator to consult with
a sample of users. In other cases full corporation approval may be required. This approach
enables an appropriate response to be documented in each case.

The other significant roles in the system will be

- System administration   Undertaken by a senior member of the College executive with administrative support. The
role will include holding regular meetings with
manual coordinators on the administration and
development of the system, notifying coordinators of policies going out of date and progress
chasing any areas which fall behind schedule.
From time to time it will also be necessary to
check that copies of the manuals, held by official
manual holders, are being kept in good order.
- Manual holders   The right to hold a set of manuals should be
restricted to designated 'manual holders'. The
number of copies in circulation should be as
small as possible whilst still ensuring that all
staff can have reasonable access. Administrative
offices, middle managers, general offices and
libraries can be useful targets. Manual holders
should be expected to display their manuals
prominently and make them available to all
staff. They should also ensure that updates
are filed quickly and the manual kept in good
order. As mentioned above, this is more likely
to be achieved if this is checked from time to
time with the manuals moved on to someone
else if the individual concerned fails to make it
a priority. In a fairly large College about forty
copies have proved to be sufficient.

Getting Started

For those of you thinking of embarking on this exercise some pointers to get you started

1   Call in all the policies, procedures, forms and guidelines in operation throughout every part of the organization. Be prepared to be entertained by the differences in approach and contradictions you unearth.
2   Organize them into a draft 'themed' manual structures.
3   Appoint a coordinator in each area.
4   Work with them to draw up a development plan for each manual listing policies to be included, areas which require development and the expected date of completion in each case. Do not be over ambitious at this stage.
5   When you have achieved 'critical mass' appoint your manual holders and launch the system.

Operating Rules

To achieve prominence and credibility throughout the institution a high quality format should be introduced throughout. The adoption of rules on presentation such as those listed below will ensure a common approach between the various coordinators involved.

SAMPLE POLICIES AND PROCEDURES MANUAL SPECIFICATION

Draft policy revisions should be sent to the Vice Principal's office before issue.
    A revised index will be supplied by the Vice Principal's office where appropriate.
    All revisions must be circulated by the coordinator according to the format described below.

FORMAT

1   All policies should carry a blank title page using the format supplied.
2   All original text should be printed in univers/helvetica or similar 12pt auto line spacing.
3   The document number must be printed in the same typeface in 15pt in the top right hand corner of every page.
4   Sheets can be either single or double sided.
5   Policies must be renewed before the due date after appropriate consultation. The maximum currency of a policy is three years.
6   The Vice-Principal's office will contact maintainers two months in advance of next revision date.

ARRANGEMENTS FOR REVIEW

Two months in advance of the revision date each policy must be reviewed by the maintainer.

Such a review normally includes seeking the views of (a sample of) the users/customer affected, the precise nature and scale of the exercise being appropriate to the nature of the policy concerned.

The process used for the review should be declared on the front sheet of each policy using the format prescribed below. This will be reviewed by the Vice Principal when the revised policy is presented for quality assurance, prior to circulation.

Maintainers seeking advice on an appropriate procedure for review should contact the Vice Principal.

Ensuring Implementation

If the system contains materials which people find useful it will be used. Its status will be enhanced if it reacts to requests for guidance material passed on by staff. It can also be given a high profile in the institution through posters, staff handbook, review procedures and your newsletter. In key areas, however, it will be necessary to check that systems are being operated effectively. This takes up into the area of systems audit which will be discussed in detail in chapter 12.

Chapter 9

Teaching and Learning

Much has been gained, in recent years, from the examination and partial adoption, of developments in quality assurance from outside the world of education. Standards, such as ISO 9000 and Investors in People, and approaches, such as TQM, have been influential contributors to the debate within education, and as such are reflected within the contents of this book. However, the underlying cultures of the organizations in which they were first developed were often very different from that which prevailed, and to some extent still exist within education. This cultural difference does not invalidate the power of these approaches, but it may have the effect of slowing down change, possibly to an unacceptable degree.

The dominance of teaching and learning is not only the raison d'être of the institution, but that which dominates the activity of the majority of its employees, singles it out for special consideration and treatment.

I will look specifically at quality in teaching and learning under the following three headings:

Quality through design
Quality in delivery
Assessment and monitoring

Quality through Design

The importance of a well designed learning experience is increasingly recognized as a key issue in improving the quality of the overall learning experience. The notion that this process itself needs to be managed, resourced and drawn into the overall planning of the institution marks a radical departure from a situation where design is best characterized as a spare time activity undertaken by individual members of staff working, for the most part, on their own.

Focusing attention on good design will provide a powerful mechanism for improving the quality of the learning experience and increasing the efficiency of the process by which that experience is delivered.

An effective design process will include the following features.

- *A managed process*

The design and development of learning provision must increasingly be recognized as part of a teacher's workload and recognized as such within their statement of responsibilities for the year. Some teachers may become more specialized at this activity and others may increasingly deliver courses and materials which have been designed for them by others. Overall, however, formal teacher contact is likely to decrease. In such circumstances how can the effectiveness of learning improve?

- *The whole learning experience*

Part of the answer must lie in better targeting of available resources and providing more structure and support to that part of the learning which takes place outside the traditional classroom. For each topic, unit or module the designer must determine and specify the best and most efficient mix of teaching and learning styles to deliver the topic in question. This could include:

— Conventional classroom activity
— Lecture format
— Home reading
— Use of College Resources Centre
— Group or individual topic research
— Use of structured learning materials
— Work-based earning
— Small group tutorial
— Instrutor supervised activity

The designer will have to bear in mind the following constraints:

- *The likely level of resources available*

In more advanced settings this will be expressed as a budget. Each of the resources chosen will have its price. The job of the designer then becomes

to achieve the best possible quality within the limits of the available resources.

- *Market demand*

Students and other stakeholders will have their own views as to what is likely to constitute an acceptable learning programme. They may be uncomfortable with unfamiliar approaches. There is no point in developing a perfect learning experience if no-one will participate in it.

- *Outcomes*

The redesigned programme must deliver the quality of results that students and other stakeholders require of it. This will normally include examination success and satisfactory retention.

The outcomes of this process will include:

- *The specification of teaching and learning styles*

By pulling together the results of this process across the institution information on teaching and support staff requirements, likely learning centre loading, investment requirements can be collected which will enable monitoring of the development and use of learning materials.

These outputs will provide valuable data for the institution's planning processes helping to determine both staffing and equipment investment strategies.

- *Ownership of learning and support materials*

You might be forgiven for comparing parts of the education system to the last days of the music hall. We have great performers doing things that people want to see, but when the performance is over what have we left to show for it? The new cinema down the road has a hit on its hands and they can show it over and over again.

The analogy is not without its point. Some of our greatest assets are effectively lost to us time and time again. They are to be found amongst the learning materials produced, discarded, locked away in cupboards or stored at home. They represent a huge investment in time, knowledge and creativity and we let it run through our fingers.

Effective learning materials have an important role to play in structuring the learning experience beyond the classroom. Institutions will wish to develop standards for the production of materials as part of their overall standards for course design.

Changes in technology are likely to turn this approach from a fringe activity into a realizable practical reality through their impact on

- *The low cost production of interactive course materials such as CD-ROM*

Interactive learning materials offer a quantum leap in the technology of course design. Schools and colleges are already making use of commercially available materials but some colleges are already investing in the technology to author and produce CD-ROM based materials for themselves. This technology will give course designers the ability to produce and customize interactive course materials as part of an overall course package. The guided use of interactive course materials will provide a powerful tool for institutionally-based learning.

- *The widespread availability of course materials for exchange or download*

There is already an apparently endless supply of learning materials available for any internet user or more conventionally through established open learning consortia and suppliers. This supply will be further enhanced by the inter-college and sector-wide broadband links already constructed or proposed. Any institution which has the technology and expertise to identify, customize and incorporate suitable learning materials into its own learning programmes will develop a significant competitive advantage for itself and enhance the programmes its offers for its students. The widespread availability of these materials for customization significantly lowers the set up costs for designers who wish to incorporate this style of learning into their programmes. This is likely to have a significant impact on the scale of future development.

- *Technology for cataloguing and administration*

The key to capturing and maintaining stocks of learning materials must be the cataloguing of course specifications, the course materials associated with them and the administration of any materials subsequently employed.

In the past it has been problematic as to whether this activity was best undertaken at section level, close to the academic staff responsible for production and revision or centrally by the library or learning resources service which could make the catalogue available for all comers.

The availability of computer networks opens up the possibility for distributed catalogues and administration whereby materials held locally can be administered centrally and made available to all through a distributed index and reservation system. Materials held on disk will be available for instant access at any location. The administration and production of materials will require its own support, either through training of existing staff or specialist appointments.

- *Course design standards*

Programme designers should not be expected to work in isolation. They should receive training for what they do, receive the support of specialist staff and the College's approvals mechanism and be provided with a set of standards which they can work to.

A sample set of course design standards is given in appendix 2.

- *Training*

The elements of a training programme could include:

— College course design standards
— Matching course design with the likely level of resources available
— Learning styles preferences in different customer groups
— Changes in learning styles and learning technology

- *Specialist support*

Many colleges have operated a Course Approvals Committee with the remit of determining whether new proposals met the standards, explicit or otherwise, determined by the College. This approach has obvious merit but it can be criticized as being both inflexible and unsupportive. It may be reasonably well suited to an annual cycle of development and review but can run into difficulties where a rapid response is required, particularly if the programme proposed does not meet with expectations.

An alternative approach has been to develop a team of senior or appropriately experienced staff into a team of 'curriculum consultants'. When a new course proposal is notified a consultant will be attached to the development team to advise on its development and, as an external member of the team, to ensure that the proposal meets course design standards.

There are many benefits to this approach. It is flexible and not time bound. The process can be as rapid or protracted as is appropriate to each case. Where minor changes to an individual module are concerned the consultant may nod it through rapidly while major new course proposals may need the attention of a number of consultants bringing together the range of specialisms required. Development teams will be glad of the assistance they receive, particularly as is the case in many submission to validating bodies, there is a great deal of commonality between their proposals and other submissions that have gone before. The approach reduces the need to reinvent the wheel.

Quality in Delivery

Improving the quality of the delivery of teaching and learning is probably the most complex issue facing any manager. It is, of course, fraught with difficulties and sensitivities. Are we even able to agree on what is meant by 'good' teaching or is the term devalued by constant shifts in educational fashion?. Worse still are we able to gather sufficient evidence on individuals or groups on which we can draw reliable conclusions.

Teaching is archetypically an activity which takes place behind closed doors. Students, particularly school leavers can be reluctant to complain, even on an official survey form and often restrict their observations to remarks about the heating, the refectory or the state of the corridors. Direct observation can only provide a snapshot, whether of a good or bad day it is difficult to tell. There has been considerable emphasis of late on the monitoring of outcomes. But to what extent are a set of outcomes directly the result of the activities of an individual teacher, how much is dependent on the institution and its policies and how much on factors beyond its reach?

Against this background TQM, with its talk of empowerment, continuous improvement and team work, can seem very attractive, but it is slow and is it enough?

The following strategies are offered to accelerate improvement in the quality of delivery;

- Accredited training;
- Appraisal;
- Discipline and competence.

Three further strategies based loosely on the assessment of teaching quality will also be examined:

- Self-assessment;
- Monitoring of outcomes;
- Inspection.

Accredited Training

For a business primarily concerned with education, which promotes the value of training as the key to economic survival and success, our record in training our own staff is fairly poor. The tradition of academic independence has been extended to cover responsibility for professional development with, until recently, each individual being left to determine their own development needs and seek to meet them as best they could.

The development of appraisal schemes and the influence of quality standards such as Investors in People has begun to change this view as institutions increasingly recognize the strategic importance of professional development and seek to influence the development agenda in line with the requirements of the business.

In further education a potentially important culture shift has taken place following the virtual imposition of Training and Development Lead Body (TDLB) awards for all involved in the assessment of NVQ and GNVQ courses. TDLB awards are an important part of the assessment quality strategy for G/NVQ. They ensure that all staff involved have received proper training to national standards so that there is sufficient confidence in their ability to assess to enable assessment to take place within the institution or the workplace without recourse to a externally supervised examination.

What the introduction of TDLB has now established, not without resistance from some quarters, is that it is perfectly proper to require teaching staff to demonstrate competence and if necessary receive training in skills which are fundamental to their ability to do the job even if those skills are to some extent covered by earlier spells of teacher training or experience on the job.

With the aim of setting and raising standards in 'core teaching skills' it should be possible to extend the TDLB approach to cover the full range of competences required to fulfil the broad requirements of the teacher's job, updating these competences as the role develops over time. This process would entail

(i) identifying the skill areas in which competence is required;
(ii) working with staff to train/accredit all staff in line with these competences.

The introduction of such a programme could be phased over time with APL being used wherever possible. Elements of the programme could be so constructed to ensure training in a wider range of approaches to learning than might have been the case when any existing teaching training qualification was completed.

A detailed skills map of jobs in the further education sector is currently being drawn up by FEDA while any education lead body would also be expected to contribute to this area. This will all help provide a framework to support such an approach. There are already a number of TDLB units which support this approach.

The same approach could be adopted in other skill areas, for example, information technology and tutorial work/interviewing.

Selecting an Approach

There are two broad approaches to implementing a universal system of accredited training. The approaches, which are not necessarily exclusive, are:

(i) appraisal-based
(ii) team-based

• *Appraisal based*

This approach is relatively straightforward. It is based on an individual discussion with each member of staff probably as an integral part of the appraisal process. The broad skill areas required to cover the individual's current and projected responsibilities would be discussed and agreed and a phased training programme mapped out leading to accreditation in all core skill areas. A proforma listing the skills areas and training modules available could help give more structure to the appraisal process and provide an output from the appraisal process which could contribute to the development of the entire staff development plan, giving a clear indication for the likely demand for each training module.

• *Team development*

In this approach the Staff Development Unit or Scheme Coordinator would work with entire staff teams rather than individual staff members. Teams could be selected according to development needs or simply at random in a phased programme which would eventually cover virtually all teaching staff. This approach offers a number of advantages in that the members of the team themselves become a resource for sharing good practice under the guidance of an external (to the team) facilitator. The process would be a considerable contribution to team development and may appear less threatening than more individually based approaches.

Appraisal

Since its introduction in further education in the early 1990s, initially as part of a nationally negotiated teaching staff pay award, full-time teaching staff appraisal has become almost universal throughout the sector, playing a vital role in supporting staff through a period of rapid development and cultural change.

Well structured schemes can perform a variety of roles including:

- identifying the development needs of staff both as individuals and contributors to institutional objectives;
- clarifying an individual's responsibilities and their role in the achievement of objectives;
- providing feedback on performance.

In many colleges these schemes have been extended to include business support staff and in some cases hourly paid part-time staff.

The essential features of an appraisal scheme are:

- training for appraisers and appraisees;
- an initial meeting to explain the process and agree the pattern of dates, times and evidence;
- evidence of performance, for example, direct observation, reports, documentation, etc. (direct observation can be structured around published institutional standards, for example, teaching standards, where available);
- a revised job description and information on likely future changes in responsibility (the appraisal interview can be used to update the job description on a regular basis);
- the appraisal interview, normally with one's line manager;
- written agreed outcomes (for example, an action plan or personal development plan);
- follow-up action and review of outcomes (this should form a part of the next scheduled appraisal but a 'mid-term' review can also be useful);
- a forum for reviewing and evaluating the appraisal process.

Some institutions have sought to link appraisal to performance related pay (PRP). PRP provides managers with the ability to focus staff attention on key objectives if they are reflected within the PRP criteria. On the other hand academic staff, in particular, tend to be less motivated by financial inducements than their colleagues in industry, moreover PRP can be a blunt-edged weapon drawing attention and effort away from issues which are not adequately represented or even foreseen in the PRP criteria.

Where a PRP scheme is in operation linking the performance review to the appraisal will increase the status of the appraisal exercise. It will also represent an efficient use of management and staff time. An important disadvantage, however, is that any discussion on personal development needs is likely to be less honest and open when the overriding aim of the exercise has become to convince one's line manager of one's performance.

Discipline and Competence

Education is an industry which depends probably more than any other on the quality and commitment of its staff. It is increasingly recognized that there are inevitability a small minority of individuals employed within the service who are unable or unwilling to provide the standards of service required in today's competitive and progressive environment.

Organizational culture has often made it difficult to confront these issues. We have been eager to develop mechanisms for support and institutional accountability, while a culture of individual responsibility has been left on the back burner. It has to be recognized that the incompetent teacher can do immeasurable damage to not only the students in direct contact, but also the institution as a whole, through damage to its reputation, its market position and the demotivation effect on other members of staff. Proper and efficient mechanisms for dealing with competence and discipline and the will to use them are important features of any quality improvement strategy.

Assessment and Monitoring

Inspection

The direct observation of teaching and learning by experienced practitioners external to the institution has provided the longest established and best known quality assessment mechanism in education.

Her Majesty's Inspectorate, comparatively infrequent visitors in most cases, have been superseded, at least in English further education and schools by the Further Education Funding Council Inspectorate and the Office for Standards in Education (OFSTED).

The Inspectorate is expected to provide a measure of accountability for the sectors by reporting on the quality of education provided by institutions primarily funded from the public purse. In addition to published reports they provide feedback to managers and staff and seek to stimulate quality improvement in institutions they have inspected through the requirement on the institution to provide action plans with follow-up visits as appropriate.

The publication of the inspection report and, in the case of further education, associated performance grades, can provide motivation for both managers and staff to improve performance.

The inspection approach is sometimes criticized on the grounds of:

- the amount of resource employed when measured against the long-term improvements in quality attributable to the inspection process;
- the distortion of an institution's own agenda due to the enormous amount of advance preparation inevitably undertaken;
- the fact that inspectors will only see a snapshot, and a highly contrived one at that, of the reality of life within a particular institution;
- the failure, at least until now, of the inspection system to encourage institutions and individuals and groups within them to take responsibility for quality for themselves.

Both the FEFC and OFSTED have published inspection frameworks to guide the process of inspection and underpin the institution's preparations for inspection.

The future of inspection

Although in further education at least it now seems likely that the current inspection process will survive for a further four-year cycle (see chapter 1) the major set piece inspection itself seems likely to be scaled down in future with more reliance placed on colleges' own quality assurance systems, where it has been demonstrated that they are sufficiently robust to inspire the necessary confidence. The role of the Corporation, as a partially independent observer of the management of the College, may also receive greater prominence. Colleges should keep these trends in mind as they prepare both for inspections in the current round and beyond.

Preparing for inspection

In view of the resources involved in the inspection process and the likely changes in emphasis outlined above it is better not just to prepare for inspection but to allow yourself sufficient time or sufficient resources to use the requirements of the inspection process, particularly the assessing achievement framework but focusing on quality improvement and the aim rather than the inspection process itself.

The following framework may help.

1   Set up a senior management group to audit College compliance with the inspection framework. Managers will need to draw on a whole range of evidence at their disposal including the outcomes of any self-assessment process.

The involvement of senior management throughout is important for both practical and symbolic reasons. The commitment of senior management to quality improvement will be an important factor.

2   In areas where you have strengths identify the documentary evidence you will wish to present to inspectors to ensure their attention.

3   In areas where you identify weaknesses draw up an action plan, identify the person and resources responsible and agree a timetable for response.

A possible format for the above is shown below:

Inspection criteria	Comment	Evidence	Action required	Who/when

4   Continue to monitor the action plan against the agreed timetable, re-negotiating as necessary.

5   Review the documentary evidence required by the Inspectorate. Agree and collect the documentation required, merging it with that which you wish to present as identified under point 2. Organize this information in an accessible readable and indexed format.

6   Draw up your 'self-assessment report' working from the audit undertaken under point 1.

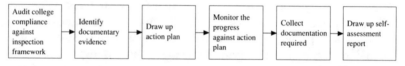

An example: Students' Recruitment, Guidance and Support

Strengths	Weaknesses	Evidence
Impartial Guidance		
The right to unbiased confidential guidance is a College Charter commitment.		College Charter
The College has a contract with Wiltshire careers guidance services to provide careers guidance on site.		Contract available
Follow-up surveys of student perception are undertaken by the Director of Student Services.		Published in College report
A licensed 'interviewer' scheme was introduced to ensure full time interviewing staff were adequately trained to perform their role.		Specification and attendance records

Strengths	Weaknesses	Evidence
APL APL is now available on most GNVQ/NVQ courses and will be extended to all areas this year. A College handbook on APL has been published to support the operation of APL throughout the College.	APL has yet to be marketed fully and demand remains at low levels.	
Induction programmes A College policy on induction has been implemented. Follow up surveys of student perception are undertaken by the Director of Student Services are undertaken.	College induction schemes are not operated uniformly across the College.	Curriculum manual
Transfer procedures Transfers are eased through the operation of a common timetable across the College.	There are relatively few cases of this facility being used for 'cross course' combinations	Curriculum manual
Access to support A College tutorial and guidance policy is in operation. All students are allocated to a tutor as a College charter commitment. Follow up surveys of student perception are undertaken by the Director of Student Services are undertaken.	Student perception of this service is patchy. There is need for continuing development in this area. College policy and materials are not used uniformly across the College.	Student administration manual tutorial handbook Published in College report
Student attendance Student attendance is monitored by the class teacher and the personal tutor. Great emphasis has	The register recording module has proved difficult to implement.	Tutorial Records

89

Strengths	Weaknesses	Evidence
been placed on the importance of retaining students.	In the absence of central data reports are compiled by the faculties.	
College support for this activity should be available through register recording and a notification of poor attendance system to be introduced this year.	Evidence of student attendance was not available in a significant number of cases.	Project Minutes
Poor retention rates are subject to faculty action plans.		Action plans available
Student rights and responsibilities All students complete a student learning agreement. This has been revised to take account of concerns, particularly in the case of adult students.		Learning agreements available
The College publishes a Charter which clearly outlines the commitments that the College makes to its students.		Charter

Further suggestions for strengthening the role for self-assessment are outlined below.

The use of internal inspection

Some colleges have responded to the onset of inspection by setting up their own 'internal inspectorates' to reproduce the effect of an inspection before the real thing arrives. This can involve relatively low key approaches such as peer appraisal, inspection by line managers or other members of the management team, the use of external consultants or arrangements with other colleges.

Internal inspection attracts both the advantages and disadvantages of the inspection system, outlined earlier, with the possible additional hazard of effectively reducing the responsibility of line managers to remain in direct touch with the quality of work produced in their area of responsibility. They should be, after all, in the best position to maintain regular contact through a variety of mechanisms and so gain an overall perspective which is far more reliable that any external snapshot.

Systems audit

An alternative and efficient alternative to full inspection can be found in a systems audit. Here a team of auditors check to ensure that key systems are being operated. The rationale for this approach being that if the systems themselves are effective and staff are operating them satisfactorily then quality will improve.

It is relatively simple to gather evidence that a system has been in operation when compared with the complex and time consuming task of direct observation. More detail on this process is given in chapter 12.

Self-assessment

A key challenge for schools and colleges is likely to be the development of honest, efficient and detailed self-assessment processes. Many approaches are, of course, possible but the mechanism I am suggesting here builds on a successful approach to institutional self-assessment described in the 'preparations for inspection' section, above, an annual team review and self-assessment described in detail in chapter 12 and the systems audit referred to above.

A possible approach

1   The annual review (sometimes called course review) be extended to include a graded self-assessment using FEFC grading definitions defined earlier.
2   This grading is undertaken at staff team level in the first instance and should include both comment and proposed grade in the following areas:

- the institution's published teaching standards (see chapter 10)
- list the main activities undertaken by the team
- the balance of skills within the team
- the overall effectiveness of staff within the team
- the ability to work as a team (see features listed in chapter 6)
- the operation of College procedures
- the quality of outcomes achieved by the team
    — exam results
    — retention
    — progression
    — service standards
    — customer satisfaction
    — financial management
    — growth in student numbers.
- other items from relevant features for the inspection framework.

Having graded each individual criteria the team would then be in a position to propose its own composite grade with a brief justification for each element provided in the comment column.

Areas of weakness would be placed on the relevant action plan.
3   Each grade would then be moderated through discussion between

the team leader and the line manager, who would in most cases, have undertaken a direct observation as part of the appraisal process.

4   A further moderation exercise would be undertaken at institutional level where there would be discussion on:

(a)   the grade awarded and the rationale behind it;
(b)   evidence for the grade awarded;
(c)   further investigation with teams where this is thought to be necessary or teams chosen at random as a control exercise. This to include direct observation where appropriate.

5   Those involved in moderation at institutional level would need to meet to discuss a selection of grades awarded after the process was complete in order to promote consistency.
6   Corporation members or and the College inspector could be invited to join the audit team or the final grading meeting.
7   The results of this process could be fed into the whole College self-assessment process described earlier.

A form of documentation to support this process is described in the context of team review and self-assessment in chapter 12.

Monitoring of outcomes

If I have satisfied customers, successful students and meet my growth targets, what am I missing? (College Principal)

In recent years there has been increasing emphasis on measuring and controlling outcomes as a means to quality improvement. League tables, the achievement of charter commitments, NVQ competences, performance indicators and the 'Publication of Information on Student Achievement (PISA)' returns are all examples of the current vogue for sampling the products of the education and presenting them as reliable indicators of the quality of the educational process itself.

It may be possible to construct the most rational, intellectually appealing, state of the art quality assurance system, without regard to whether it actually succeeds in improving the chances and the performance of the customers it seeks to serve. It is equally dangerous, however to assume that education is akin to a simple mechanical system, and that failure to hit a target or other indicator can necessarily be corrected at operational level in a simple cause and effect relationship.

Education abounds with simplistic quality assurance systems which seek to 'correct' a poor set of results through exhorting staff to 'do something about it'. Staff obviously have a vital role to play, but equally they may already be doing all in their power, and the root of the problem may lie outside their sphere of influence. Deming illustrates this with his 'beads' experiment which is used to show that even in a simple random process there is considerable statistical variation, totally beyond the control of the operator. The effect of exhortation may be only to reduce self-esteem, reduce motivation and reduce quality.

We cannot, however, ignore outcomes altogether. If we do our quality assurance processes become a meaningless and closed intellectual exercise. We must analyze our results while understanding their limitations and seek to interpret them as best we can as indicators for future action.

Although achievement at individual course level may be highly erratic and difficult to target, the larger the sample, the more statistical validity it will have. It may be fruitful to look at large aggregations of results at departmental or institutional level or examine long term trends smoothing out unrepresentative 'blips' in the data.

The above argument supports the following approach:

- analyze and scrutinize as wide a range of outcome data as your systems and resources will permit (choosing a system of performance indicators is dealt with in more detail in chapter 10);
- recognize that any one data element based on a small sample will be subject to statistical variation outside the control of any individual teacher;
- notwithstanding the above outcomes need to maintain at least as high a profile within the institution as they will be given without;
- ask teams for comment or proposed action on their results rather than demanding a knee jerk reaction everytime something appears to go wrong;
- targets and standards can be set at institutional level, but be cautious about interpreting them mechanically down to course team level. The effect may be demotivating and produce the opposite of what you intend. Remember that outcomes can at best tell you what has already happened.

Internal verification

Internal verification is the process by which standards of institution-based assessment are assured in NVQ, GNVQ and their Scottish equivalent. It is linked to the achievement of the Training and Development Lead Body (TDLB) awards referred to earlier.

An internal verification system will aim to provide evidence that national standards are being achieved to external verifiers, moderators and examiners. It will also provide staff with the opportunity to monitor the quality of delivery of learning and assessment.

The personnel involved in an internal verification structure may include:

- The Assessor (any member of the staff team involved in assessment activity);
- The Programme Team Verifier:

  — provides advice and support to the assessor team;
  — ensures systematic records are kept;
  — ensures regular meetings of the team are held;
  — assists assessors in ensuring the quality of assessment design;
  — liaises with the Internal Verifier Coordinator in training, planning key activities and ensuring consistent sampling of units and assessments;
  — enables assessor teams to sample and evaluate each other's assessment evidence by multimarking and team sampling exercises;
  — completes awarding body certification;
  — liaises with External Verifier.

- The Internal Verifier Coordinator:

  — coordinates internal verification within a broad subject area;
  — ensures assessors and team verifiers possess all necessary documentation;
  — monitors verification practice within the subject area;
  — ensures assessors and team verifiers are kept up to date with changes in procedure;
  — obtains information from students on assessor practice and ensures access to an appeals procedure.

- The Centre Verifier:

  — coordinates and monitors institutional internal verification procedures;
  — ensure the development of the internal verification systems;
  — liaises with external verifiers when issues arise.

Internal verification is more that just an assessment system. The interdependence of assessment and the achievement of competence, particularly in an actual or realistic work environment, is so close that quality assurance of the assessment process inevitably strengthens the process of delivery.

Internal verification seeks to improve quality through ensuring adherence to standards and requiring teamwork, sampling, adherence to procedures and close supervision.

Chapter 10

Targets and Standards

The British education system has become increasingly focused on outcomes. This manifests itself in:

- qualifications such as NVQ specified in terms of competence;
- funding models which increasingly reward achievement of the qualification at the expense of funding the process itself;
- services which are specified in terms of a pre-determined set of operational standards;
- operational and strategic plans which written in terms of the precise objectives to be achieved.

Hand in hand with such developments has come an increasing emphasis on the setting and measuring of targets and standards. This approach can take many forms, for example:

- numerical targets — for student enrolment, examination success, retention, client satisfaction etc.;
- 'SMART' (Specific, Measurable, Achievable, Relevant, Time constrained) objectives — for development actions;
- standards — for services provided.

These can be set at institutional, section, team or individual level.

This approach has brought with it a significant number of benefits.

- It provides a clear set of goals for those expected to implement them.
- It is possible for the organization and its stakeholders to measure progress against its expectations from one year to the next.
- It allows progress to be reviewed, a process which will itself suggest a framework for further action.
- It provides a framework to support delegation and empowerment.
- It is much easier to monitor the achievement of targets than the quality of the processes that lead to them.
- A framework of objectives, targets and standards can be used to coordinate the activity of the whole organization.

- If the process of determining them is participative the organization can gain a more realistic view as to what it is possible to achieve.
- For some individuals in some circumstances it can provide motivation.

There are, however, some disadvantages, in particular:

- it is not always possible to foresee all development actions required in advance, clearer objectives may emerge during the planning period;
- attention may be focused on the need to complete objectives at the expense of work on other emerging issues, reducing the ability of the organization to respond flexibly;
- the achievement of objectives, standards and targets may depend on factors beyond the control of those charged with meeting them;
- some individuals or groups find specific objectives or targets demotivating and work better in a holistic, self motivating and creative environment. Many of the organization's better motivated staff may fall into this category;
- managers may use targets as a means of passing over responsibility and give insufficient attention as to how they might be realized. At worst they may fall into a sense of false security believing a target set is a target achieved.

In summary, exposure to targets, objectives and standards is inevitable and brings many benefits to the organization but they should be used with caution, in particular.

- progress should be reviewed regularly with a flexible attitude taken to changes in circumstances;
- managers should see target setting as the beginning not the end of the process of achieving them;
- some individuals or groups should be allowed to work in a less constrained environment;
- staff should not be made solely responsible for factors outside their control;
- those expected to deliver should always be consulted on the level of any target to be set.

On this last point a useful distinction can be made between quality criteria, a feature for which a quality standard should be set, and the quality standard itself, being the specific level or numerical value adopted in each case. The former may legitimately be set by the organization and have a 'long shelf life', while staff will be more involved in setting the exact level of the standard, which may vary from one year to the next.

Having dispensed with the health warnings here are some practical examples of criteria and standards which you may wish to use or adapt to your own circumstances.

Teaching Standards

As the primary activity of the organization it will be useful to derive a set of standards which indicate the organization's view of what constitutes good practice. Such prescription goes right to the heart of the self-image of a professional and therefore the process of implementation will need to be handled sensitively with wide consultation within the institution advisable. The list which follows should provide you both with useful ideas and source material.

1   *Course programme*

A published course programme is distributed to staff and students, to include:

- induction policy and programme;
- arrangements for APL;
- tutorial programme;
- rights and responsibilities;
- equal opportunities policy;
- key issues in health and safety;
- subjects and major topics;
- core units;
- options available;
- names of staff responsible and contact details;
- course weekly, termly and annual timetable;
- assignment programme and deadlines for submission and feedback;
- access to learning resources;
- dates of examinations and assessments;
- details of the award and awarding body;
- assessment and appeals policy;
- work experience policy and practice;
- arrangements for transfer between programmes;
- routes for progression.

2   *Teaching/learning*

- Learning sessions start on time.
- Timetabled sessions are always appropriately managed.
- The study programme has been planned by the course team.
- The aims and objectives of the programme are specified.
- Study programmes aim to extend skills and encourage personal development and group work.
- Study programmes demonstrate appropriate integration of study skills.
- Core skills are integrated when appropriate.
- Study programmes include a range of different teaching and learning methods.

- The range is apparent within each day, week, term and year of the learning programme.
- Study programmes proceed at an appropriate pace and level.
- Resources are appropriate and well prepared.
- Practical activities are conducted competently and safely.
- The equal opportunities policy is reflected by good classroom practice.
- The range of methods and resources takes account of the different learning needs of individuals.
- In particular, the arrangements should enable students with special learning needs to participate.
- Learning achievement is continuously monitored.
- Assignment deadlines are adhered to.
- Routine work is returned with formative feedback within two weeks.
- Major assignments and projects are returned with comments/grades within one month.
- The assessment programme covers all aims and objectives.
- Assessment opportunities are prepared for and planned with the student.
- Assessment is at the appropriate standard.
- Assessment decisions are shared with the student.
- Assessors and internal verifiers are appropriately trained.
- Internal verification procedures follow college quality standards.
- Assessment appeals are responded to quickly and effectively (according to policy).
- A formative record of achievement for each student is maintained.
- Individual progress is discussed with the student at least once a term.
- A written report and action plan is negotiated and shared with the student each term.
- A summative Record of Achievement is produced at the end of the course or programme.
- Class and course surveys are conducted and the results discussed and negotiated.
- Attendance is monitored and absences followed up by personal contact after no more than three absences.

3 Tutoring

The tutor:
- publishes the tutorial programme and negotiates it with students;
- attends tutor training sessions;
- completes the Learning Agreement with each student;
- keeps records of group and individual tutorials;
- monitors and records the development of personal skills;
- gives information on college facilities and resources for example, counselling and welfare, college calendar, refectory services, learning resources service;

- gives guidance on career progression and information sources;
- monitors reports;
- works with the student each term to produce and update the personal development or action plan;
- negotiates and records individual timetables and subsequent changes and modifications.

The above list incorporates most of the ideas included in the further education inspection framework.

It can effectively be brought to the attention of staff through its inclusion in the self-assessment process (chapter 12 and appendix 2) whereby teams are required to assess their own performance against an abbreviated version of the standard.

Elements requiring attention can then be transferred to an action plan.

It can also be used to:

- support managers when observing teaching sessions (for example, as part of the appraisal process);
- provide a framework to underpin investigations regarding teaching competence.

Service Standards

It is evidently more complex to set up a system of service standards for non-teaching activities. Colleges have used quality teams, user groups and service providers to draw up and agree systems of standards, area by area until all major College services are covered.

Those looking for a quicker, though obviously less thorough, approach might:

- ask each area to propose a system of quality indicators and standards for key aspects of its work;
- publish the proposals for consultation with user;
- debate the proposals in an appropriate forum, for example, management team or Academic Board;
- adopt, implement and review.

The provision of evidence for the achievement of service standards can be undertaken centrally, but it is often more effective and efficient for the services themselves to be charged with the responsibility to provide evidence — on a sample basis if necessary — that the standards are being met. In this way they are continually reminded of the need to achieve them and the whole exercise acquires a developmental aspect, helping to justify the resource which must be committed to it.

Service standards can be published in the institutional plan or in a 'funding agreement' as described in the next section.

Service Standards — an example

Finance

Management accounts	Within ten working days
Sales/invoice raising	Within twenty-one days of receipt of information by Finance
Supplier payments	100 per cent within due date where invoices processed accurately and on time
Process 'agreed' internal transfers	Within the month of receipt
Budgets into Dolphin	By the time first management accounts issued
Appropriately completed claims processed by payroll	100 per cent by the payroll deadline
Manual cheque requisitions	Within two working days

Premises

Completion of routine maintenance requests	100 per cent within agreed timescale
Respond to routine requests	Within five working days
Notification of disruption	Seven days

Office Services

Turnaround of print room requests	Within three days
Respond to minor caretaking requests on working days at any time	Within one hour
Collect, sort and deliver internal mail	Twice daily
Frank and prepare external mail	Daily
Clean all areas during term-time	Daily
Rectify reported telephone faults	Within two days
Delivery of central stores items:	
ex stock	Within one day
out-of-stock	Within five days

Internal Funding Agreements

Where delegated budgets are in operation it will be useful for both parties to spell out in writing the exact terms and conditions under which funding is provided. This will provide an opportunity to clarify the amount of funding provided and any link to performance, be it in terms of student numbers or the achievement of quality standards. Information on clawback arrangements for underachievement or bonus payments for results in excess of target can also be provided. A funding agreement can prove a powerful mechanism for concentrating attention on a few key performance and quality targets. The exact choice of criteria will of course be a function of your own development agenda, the following examples may help to clarify the idea.

Example of a Funding Agreement for an Academic Section

The Faculty will receive the following recurrent funding during the academic year to sustain its operations in delivery and development subject to the conditions listed in section B.

Section A — Funding

FEFC Tariff Related =

The funding includes entry and achievement elements and allowance for remission but does not include 'ring fenced' income or funding for additional support.

HEFC(E)   =
Fully Costed (target) =
Other income   =

It is anticipated that the Faculty will make every effort to operate within the above budget but if this should prove impossible an additional grant of up to will be made available to you on condition that plans for the elimination of this deficit are brought forward during the year in line with budget projections outlined by the Director of Finance and Resources.

Section B — Targets

1   Achieving a level of enrolments equivalent to FEFC tariff units (excluding additional support).

2   Limiting student drop out to no more than 8 per cent per term.
3   At least 80 per cent of completing students achieving their target qualifications.
4   All new vocational courses being approved by the Director of Curriculum.

Failure to achieve the above (pt 1–4) will result in clawback at the full internal rate.

5   HEFC(E) enrolments of

Failure to achieve the above will result in the clawback of the relevant proportion of the funding awarded for this purpose.

6   Demonstrating the existence of, or plans for achieving, flexible entry points and modes of attendance for all GNVQ & NVQ courses.
7   Achieving an average point score of for 16–18-year-old students taking at least two 'A' levels (using PISA definitions).
8   Achieving a minimum average pass rate for 16–18-year-olds following GNVQ and precursor courses (using PISA definitions).
9   Achieving % of full and part-time staff undergoing appraisal during 1995/6.

Section C — Other points

1   Faculties exceeding their FE unit target will receive additional funding at the full demand lead rate of £6.50/unit.
2   Faculties not in receipt of net 'top up' grant will be able to 'rollover' unspent balances to the next financial year at least for funding capital purchases.

Example of a Funding Agreement for a Service Section

The Directorate will receive the following funding during the academic year 1996–97 to sustain its operations in delivery and development subject to the conditions listed in section B.

Section A — Funding

Section B — Conditions

1   The provision of a satisfactory level of services in the following areas:

Curriculum development
Learning resources

Personnel
Staff development

2 Providing evidence that the service standards listed below have been met or exceeded.

Curriculum and staff development	
Response to telephone queries from internal and external customers	Maximum two working days to respond
Response to written requests for support	Maximum one week to respond
Provide summary of activity by division/unit	Termly
Response to course notifications in accordance with curriculum procedures	Within seven days
Curriculum consultants assigned to all new courses	Within fourteen days
Supply relevant new course information to Student Services	Monthly new course update provided to Student Services Manager
Maintain quality validation procedures and curriculum policies	Dated entries in the curriculum policy and procedures manual

Learning Resources

Counter response	Within three minutes
Response to information enquiries	Within negotiated timescale
Induction sessions booked and delivered	Within one month
AVA response to telephone queries	Within two days

Personnel Services

Response time for internal and external telephone queries	Maximum two working days for initial response
Response time for internal and external correspondence	Maximum five working days for initial response
Issuing of holding letters	Maximum two working days following receipt of appointment instructions
Issue of contracts of employment	Normally a maximum four working weeks following receipt of appointment instructions. Normally six working weeks for an appointment requiring police clearance. Maximum of one working week for transfer to another contract.

3   The College achieving its enrolment target as listed in the Strategic Plan.

Unspent balances at the end of the financial year can be 'rolled over' at least for the purposes of capital expenditure.

External Targets and Standards

National Targets for Education and Training (NTET)

The establishment of national targets for skill levels within the UK population is both a recognition of, and a contribution to, the perceived importance of education and training to our ability to compete in the world economy. That the Government has chosen to express such targets largely in terms of educational outcomes is also a significant feature of the trends discussed earlier in the chapter. NTET (and their Scottish equivalent ASCETT) have been recently revised and are now set at:

	1990	1995	Target 2000
Foundation Target 1– % 19-yr-olds with NVQ 2 or equivalent	52	68	85
Foundation Target 2– % 19-yr-olds with NVQ 2 in key skills*	n/a	n/a	75
% 21-yr-olds with NVQ 3 in key skills	0	n/a	35
Foundation Target 3– % 21-yr-olds with NVQ 3 or equivalent	31	44	60
Lifetime Target 1– % of the workforce with NVQ 3 or equivalent	29	41	60
Lifetime Target 2– % of the workforce with NVQ 4 or above	17	24	30
Lifetime Target 3– % of organizations with 200+ staff gaining IIP	0	11	70
% of organizations with 50+ staff gaining IIP	0	5	35

* Communications, numeracy and IT
(Information supplied by the National Advisory Council of Education and Training Targets, July 1996)

The implications of NTET for quality management include:

- a continued emphasis on achieving qualification outcomes as an indicator of quality;
- likely continued use of funding mechanisms to encourage the achievement of national targets;
- increasing emphasis on output related funding.

Output Related Funding

Output related funding is increasingly used in education as part of a strategy to improve 'value for money' in terms of the number of positive outcomes per pound. The school sector has been so far immune to this trend but the further education funding mechanism contains an element (approximately 10 per cent) of funding dependent on the achievement of the intended qualification while a number of Training and Enterprise Council contracts have extracted an even higher proportion, up to 100 per cent in some cases.

Output related funding does have the effect of concentrating the attention of organizations, and sometimes their staff, on the need to achieve the target qualification or other prescribed outcome (for example, a job) but there are disadvantages. These include:

- reduced emphasis on broader educational objectives, for example, personal development and related studies;
- pressure to select students or trainees who are more likely to complete the programme successfully or in the shortest possible time at the expense of those who need more help, perhaps over a longer period;
- a tendency to place students on a safe programme, rather than one which might stretch them;
- pressure to complete programmes of study, even though they may no longer be the best option for the student;
- pressure to pick up unnecessary qualifications as part of the learning programme in order to maximize funding to the organization;
- pressure to complete a course of study in the shortest possible time, without regard to broader development needs;
- pressure on the organization to compromise standards, where possible, to maximize the number of qualifications awarded.

Smaller organizations, or those with a high proportion of output funding, may also experience difficulties with cash flow. This can have the effect of increasing the risks of entering a new subject area reducing overall responsiveness.

Publication of Information on Student Achievement

Increased pressure for accountability and an environment which values parental choice and a customer orientation have led to moves for more information on school and college performance to be placed in the public domain. The performance tables and more comprehensive 'Publication of Information of Student Achievement (PISA)' regulations being the most prominent indicators available to date. The performance tables include information on average point scores for GCSE, 'A' level, GNVQ advanced and now GNVQ intermediate students, while PISA regulations require data on a full range of qualifications analyzed by age band, programme area and, where possible, grade performance as well as collecting information on student destinations.

The information provides, for the first time, a limited picture of the progress of each institution, and the education service as a whole, if only in terms of the indicators used against the indicators used. As with all performance indicators they can only give a partial view of organizational effectiveness. They are, of course, liable to be interpreted far more widely.

A key feature, not so far incorporated in the performance tables, is the concept of 'value added', or distance travelled by the student during his/her course of study. Some work has been done on comparing success rates at

'A' level with GCSE grades on entry. So far it appears that there may be a reasonable correlation between grades on entry and likely 'A' level success, but no clear link has been found for vocational qualifications. The lack of a suitably robust and reliable methodology has dampened down interest in this area.

Charters

As part of the Citizen's Charter Initiative colleges are required to produce and publish charters which detail the commitments they make to their students and other stakeholders. The Charter is perceived in official circles as an important document with a key role to play in Government strategy for raising the standards of public services. The charter, and the institution's ability to live up to its commitments, will, for example, play a significant part in any future inspection.

A recent survey by Further Education Funding Council (1996) inspectors concluded that colleges had put a great deal of energy and commitment into developing charters with most colleges placing responsibility for the charter in the hands of senior managers.

Despite this it was found:

- not all students receive a copy, understand their entitlements or appreciate how charters can be used;
- some of the charter entitlements are not met effectively;
- although complaints procedures had improved systems for tracking them and monitoring progress were sometimes inadequate.

Charters could be improved by:

- converting general statements into standards that are more focused and precise;
- developing more effective monitoring and reporting arrangements.

The style of each charter varies considerably with some institutions adopting a highly descriptive style giving detailed information of their aims on a variety of issues, while others restrict themselves to specific achievable commitments often in 'bullet pointed' form. It is, in my view, this latter format which is more likely to have an effect.

The arguments over the likely effectiveness of charters broadly follow those for and against the use of tightly defined targets and standards, many of which have already been described.

In particular the publication of a charter commitment will tend to concentrate the attention of management, at least, on the commitments made. Management will therefore tend to select:

(i)   standards that are achievable;

(ii)   issues which can be expressed in specific or measurable terms.

Health service commitments, for example, have been credited with assisting in a reduction in waiting times, a key political issue when such an approach was first devised. However, they have been criticized for having little to say about the more subjective aspects involved in the quality of patient care.

Other problems centre on the attitudes of both staff and the students themselves. Staff may not see the importance of the charter with the same intensity of College managers and fail to keep themselves up to date with all but the most basic commitments. Students may show even less interest. Which of us can honestly claim to have taken on board all the various charter commitments made by the utility companies, local governments offices and others? We should not be too surprised if our customers fail to give the charter the prominence we would wish.

The contribution made by the charter to quality improvement will vary according to individual circumstances. Managers will have to balance the likely effect of the charter in this regard with the level of resources they commit to it. As an initiative on its own it may be too selective, too remote from both staff and customers and ultimately too 'top down' to fit comfortably into a total quality strategy.

By now most institutions will have published their charters. Many, however, will be seeking to review them. To do this they will need to gather information on their success in meeting existing charter commitments.

This can be accomplished through direct investigation on each point or by a sample customer perception survey.

The mechanisms for drawing up and revising your charter will be a matter for each institution, you may, however, wish to consider the following:

- draw up a timetable allowing time for consultation with staff, students, employers, schools and other stakeholders;
- allow time for discussion and approval by the governors/college corporation;
- integrate the charter as far as possible with existing institutional processes. There will be overlaps with the commitments made in the strategic plan and quality assurance mechanisms;
- ensure feedback from the charter review is fed into the strategic planning process.

Benchmarking

Benchmarking is potentially an extremely powerful mechanism for improving standards and encouraging development. In essence it involves comparing the performance of one's own institution in one aspect of its work with a leader in the field and using that comparison to determine how a similar level of performance can be achieved.

There is increasing interest in statistical comparisons as more detailed data on sector institutions becomes available through the funding councils or other agencies, but statistical comparisons are notoriously difficult to make without the ability to place the information in context.

Where possible long-term relationships, involving personal contact, should be encouraged to enable a clear understanding of the circumstances and key differences between the institutions to emerge. Despite incorporation further education institutions are still relatively open to each other and still willing to help, but remember that 'the best of breed' may lie outside the educational sector where the fact that you pose no direct competitive threat may open doors for you.

Benchmarking can be set up at institutional level, but there is considerable value in a variety of such arrangements taking place at all levels throughout the organization. The effect of each staff team, on both the teaching and non-teaching sides, identifying, twinning and visiting a leader in their own particular field can be electrifying. The benefits of observing other professionals achieving excellence in similar circumstances to their own can spark considerable creativity and motivation amongst staff, observing their peers being more convincing and effective than mere management exhortation.

Performance Indicators

Performance indicators give you a measured snapshot of a number of key indicators of the current performance of the institution itself or any part of it. They do not, and cannot, tell you everything about it. Whether they tell you enough depends on what you need to know and the relevance of the system of indicators you have chosen.

Any number of systems are possible and the choice of indicators will be informed by:

- the characteristics of the organization which are key indicators of its health and development;
- the validity of the indicators you have chosen as proxies for the above;
- the availability of reliable information to enable these indicators to be calculated.

The Further Education Funding Council in its publication, *Measuring Achievement* (FEFC, 1994) identifies the following indicators in line with the inspection framework outlined in the Circular *Assessing Achievement.*

1 College effectiveness	% achievement of funding agreement
2 College responsiveness	% growth in enrolments
3 Student responsiveness	Completion rates
4 Student achievements	% of enrolled students achieving primary learning goals
5 Contribution to national targets	Number of students achieving NTET qualifications
6 Value for money	Average level of funding per unit

The indicators offer consistency with the inspection process and reinforce a quality improvement agenda already set out in *Assessing Achievement*. The information to support them will largely be available from existing sources. The validity of indicators 1, 2 and 3 as evidence for that which is implied in their titles has however been much criticized.

Other agencies have taken a different approach. The equivalent Scottish Office publications, *Measuring Up* (1992) and *Quality and Efficiency* have identified

- student achievement ratio
- post-course success ratio
- client satisfaction
- quality of teaching and learning profile
- unit costs profile

as key indicators of organizational and sectoral health.

Institutions wishing to draw up their own performance indicator strategies may wish to consider:

- the requirements of major funding bodies;
- their own aims and/or assessment of critical success factors

in the context of the three factors listed above.

A sample performance indicator strategy based on critical success factors is given below.

1 *Introduction*

There must be evidence that the strategy for quality monitoring and enhancement includes the collection and systematic use of performance indicators. (*Assessing Achievement*, FEFC Circular 93/28)

The College requires a systematic set of performance indicators to:

- enable the setting of improvement targets and to chart progress towards them;
- support and enable the College's policy of continuous improvement based on the activity of staff teams;
- satisfy the requirements of outside agencies;
- address the education, service and business needs of the College.

The performance indicators policy will inform college data strategy and the development of the College management information system under the direction of the Head of Information Development. It takes account of the comments received to the Consultation Paper, *Proposed Performance Indicators* circulated last year.

The system of indicators should be:

- the minimum required for an accurate picture of College activity to be portrayed;
- focused on key elements;
- derived from reliable data with a minimum of administrative effort;
- provide for year-on-year comparisons;
- provide for flexibility as College aims and objectives develop.

It is recommended that indicators be developed to cover the following areas:

(i)   The achievement of College critical success factors.
(ii)   The achievement of special features of the College plan.
(iii) The continuous improvement in quality based on the activity of staff teams.
(iv) The requirements of outside agencies.

2   *Sample indicators*

All indicators should be available at course/team/division/faculty/College level as appropriate and as information systems developments permit.

(i)   The achievement of college critical success factors

(a)   Course programme

- The number of new course approvals.
- The number of programmes offering flexible entry and exit points.
- The number of programmes offering Accreditation of Prior Learning.
- The number of new programmes offered in target market segments (for example, 16–19 full-time, women returners, employer sponsored training, etc.).
- The number of new programmes offered in target industrial sectors (for example, retail, security etc.)

(b)   Recruitment

- Student application to enrolment conversion rate.
- Full-time, part-time, full-time equivalent (FTE) students enrolled with tariff conversion.
- Enrolments by market segment

See also FEFC indicators college responsiveness and college effectiveness.

(c)   Quality outcomes

- Student success and destination rates (exam entry/result), for example, using PISA and DfEE 'league table' format at course, team, division, faculty or College level.
- Student completion rate (FEFC 'student responsiveness').
- Percentage year 1 reenrolling to year 2.
- Student attendance by course, team, division, faculty.
- Percentage compliance with College quality procedures (see quality audit team, chapter 12).
- Internal customer satisfaction with College services.
- Customer satisfaction.
- Employer satisfaction.
- Achievement of 'service standards'.

See also FEFC indicators 'student achievements' and 'contribution to national targets'.

Value-added mechanisms which compare examination performance on entry with achievement on completing the course may also be used, or at least kept under review until a reliable methodology is developed.

(d)   Sound finance

The financial data required at institutional level is a matter for accounting regulations and the funding bodies[1]. Internal cost centres may benefit from a knowledge of:

- total income
- total expenditure
- surplus/deficit
- cost/successful student to course level.

(e)   Information

A wide range of indicators is possible. Levels of general information may be determined through:

- newsletter readership surveys
- employee satisfaction index.

The technical performance of the information systems may also be sampled through the list of 'service standards' (examples of service standards are given in chapter 10).

(f)   Staffing

In addition to the requirements of funding bodies (for example, FEFC staff individualized record) indicators such as the staff-student ratio and average contact hours may still have a place.

Perhaps more relevant would be net income/staff member.

Other indicators such as:

- percentage undergoing appraisal (FT and PT).
- percentage on 'flexible' contract.

may be relevant.

(ii)   The achievement of special features of the college plan

In addition to the indicators specifically linked to critical success factors, other issues may achieve prominence within day-to-day operation and as such justify the development and calculation of their own indicator. Examples might include:

- performance measures to support the College's space utilization strategy;
- performance measures to monitor the achievement of the College's equal opportunities policy.

Other measures to support the achievement of key development concerns would be determined on an annual basis as part of the College planning process.

(iii)   The continuous improvement of quality based on the activity of staff teams

If your quality policy takes the view that quality is best improved by staff teams accepting responsibility for quality improvement then it follows that teams themselves must have a role in identifying performance indicators and quality targets for themselves. The team review and self-assessment documentation included in this publication provides an opportunity for this to be formalized as staff teams set their own quality indicators and targets according to the requirements of their action plans.

(iv)   The requirements of outside agencies

Most public sector institutions will be subject to the requirements of one main funding body, but there will be others. Their requirements may differ significantly but should not be ignored. Examples may include the local Training and Enterprise Council, the Local Education Authority, the Higher Education Funding Councils and European funding agencies.

There have been attempts to draw at least some of these agencies into a single system, notably the Scottish Quality Management System, discussed earlier, but as in all elements of quality strategy the key message is to keep in mind:

- what you are trying to achieve
- what you think will work for you

and then adapt or extend this framework to satisfy, as best you can, the diverse and sometimes conflicting requirements of other agencies. Avoid, if you can, being pulled in one direction after another and thereby creating a large and incoherent system which will provide nothing but data for others.

Note

1   Details for the English Further Education Sector are given in Circular 96/13 Financial Returns, FEFC, June 1996.

Chapter 11

Client Satisfaction Surveys

The use of client surveys to establish levels of student or employer satisfaction or gather information on a range of other issues is now well established. In some colleges surveys of internal customers are undertaken as a recognition of the need to provide services of an acceptable standard to avoid breaking any link in 'the quality chain'.

A wide range of models are available and increasingly colleges are developing their own approaches as they focus in on particular areas, in line with the overall development of their quality strategy.

In this chapter I shall concentrate on reviewing the underlying issues to help you decide between competing approaches. An illustrative set of proformas is provided in appendix 3.

Structured or Unstructured?

Most, if not all, of the published formats involve a structured 'tick box' approach. These are simple to analyze and encourage the respondent to give an opinion on a pre-determined range of issues.

Such an approach, however, directs attention towards those issues which the institution, rather than the customer, feels is important. It invites an unconsidered, immediate response which may not be truly representative of underlying opinion.

An unstructured survey essentially asks the respondent to identify what, if anything is important to them by phrasing questions in the form of:

- name two things you like about the course;
- name two things that you think we could do better.

Note the request for positive feedback. Accentuating the positive can be equally as valuable as unearthing difficulties. The responses in this case will be more considered as they require a certain amount of thought beforehand. Issues undreamed of by the organization will be brought out and will provide valuable material for further discussion. Analyzing the responses to determine recurring themes and messages will, however, be time consuming. In addition, some students may not themselves take too kindly to this approach, as it requires some considerable effort to think of something to say.

A compromise between the two approaches is offered in appendix 3. Here a relatively short 'tick box' section is matched by a one which encourages local customization, for example, by the lecturer or course tutor, and a space for the student to write in his/her own observations.

Another possible compromise can be developed from the repertory grid[1] technique which has been developed to enable organizations to quantify the changes in staff attitudes that result from a programme of education or training. In this approach a series of interviews would be held with a representative sample of the client group to determine the issues which were most important to them. The issues identified could then be used to survey the views of a wider sample using a more conventional proforma approach.

This mechanism combines elements of a client driven agenda with the efficiency of a more conventional approach.

Validity

There is some evidence that younger students, in particular, are reluctant to criticize teachers or teaching styles, even in an anonymous survey. Soft targets, such as the state of decoration or the car park, often figure prominently in the issues raised.

In work on student retention recently undertaken by the Further Education Development Association (FEDA), attention was drawn to the inadequacy of the first response. When asked their reasons for leaving the course students would at first point to causes external to the institution, such as financial difficulties, pressure at home etc. When follow-up interviews were undertaken and issues probed in more depth the attitudes of the college and its staff come through as the dominant issue. The message is clear. A proforma survey can tell you just so much but if you want to gain more than a superficial impression you will have to get involved in dialogue.

Centrally or Locally Administered?

The first surveys were almost entirely College-wide initiatives. They were heavily structured and provided a great deal of information to managers who then sat round and wondered what they could do about it. One temptation in such circumstances would be to adopt a more directive management style now armed with the apparently certain knowledge of knowing what customers want. This approach does not sit very easily with the notion of empowering staff or TQM.

As far as any detailed survey work on classroom activity is concerned I favour a local approach with information fed back to classroom teachers and course teams. It then becomes the responsibility of the team to react to feedback received, discuss the issues involved and modify the approach and learning programme as appropriate to do so. A mature team may be able to accomplish this without resorting to a formal survey, relying instead on regular discussion sessions. The reluctance of many students to speak out on these occasions should, of course, be considered. Where issues arise which are beyond the competence of the team, staff should have access to the College planning process to enable any request to be at least considered. Teams operating a form of delegated budget will be able to deal promptly with many issues at local level.

Management need not therefore seek detailed information though the survey system, at least in areas where there is no cause for concern. It can discharge its responsibilities through:

- ensuring that a survey system is being operated by each team (see section on quality audit chapter 12);
- checking whether there is broad satisfaction with each course;
- investigating in more detail only when there is 'cause for concern'.

In these circumstances it is useful to have a College scheme for staff to use 'off the shelf', but teams should not be discouraged from developing their own approaches providing they meet overall institutional criteria. The ownership they feel for the system may far outweigh any flaws in overall design.

Topic Range

Providing the results are viewed in context it can be useful to survey the opinions of both staff and students on a range of different issues, to assist in policy formation and the targeting of resources.

Rather than constructing larger and larger client survey systems it is probably better to break them down into a number of different topic-based surveys each taking one particular issue and working with only a sample of the client group involved. Issues might include:

- the usefulness of induction;
- the effectiveness of tutorials;
- College success in meeting charter commitments;
- the refectory service;
- the library;
- staff perception of the College as an employer.

Dealing with Complaints

Conventional quality management literature often stresses the importance of dealing effectively with complaints. The main points made being:

- for every dissatisfied customer who complains there are many more who have not bothered to do so. They are however complaining to their friends and neighbours about you;
- dealing effectively with a complaint can be an effective way of gaining customer loyalty.

Put together these statements imply:

1 We should encourage people to complain to us when they have a grievance.
2 We should be as effective as possible in dealing with them.

Systems for dealing with complaints will necessarily vary from one institution to the next but the key elements would seem to be as follows:

- a well publicized and accessible method for making a complaint such as telephone hot line or the College reception areas;
- a central complaints logging system;
- someone to coordinate the response to each complaint and chase progress;
- a system of complaints 'case managers' to take ownership and deal with all aspects of each individual complaint (no complainant should be bounced from one part of the organization to the next);
- a service standard for response time which is shared with each complainant;
- a system of management reports on trends and issues.

The existence of a complaints procedure and ways of accessing it will normally be included in the organization's Charter.

Note

1 The Repertory Grid Technique has been developed by Dr Pamela Denicolo at the University of Reading, Department of Community Studies.

Chapter 12

Review and Self-assessment

Course review systems are now an established feature in many schools and colleges. They represent potentially the most significant and powerful mechanism in any quality management system. They provide the opportunity for staff to confront the lessons of the previous year and plan for improvements in the forthcoming session.

In this chapter I will:

- explore the link between arrangements for review and systems for planning and budgeting;
- discuss the use of the review and self-assessment to strengthen the team approach for both teaching and business support staff;
- outline a mechanism for embedding the operation of team review within the organization.

Quality and Planning

At each review all teams are faced with a set of resourcing decisions, even if the only resource they have at their disposal is where they will put their own efforts over the coming year.

Each team should ask itself the following:

1 What is the best quality we can achieve within the limits of the resources made available to us?

This is a question that teams are best able to answer for themselves. Their detailed knowledge of their own area of operation gives them the best overview of what should be done amongst all the things that could be done.

2 How could resources within the institution be better deployed to enhance quality?

This is a different issue and needs to be treated separately from the first, otherwise the answer to all quality issues tends to become, 'If only we had more resources'. Question 1 is about seeking the maximum possible quality from existing resources, which goes right to the heart of our professional duty;

question 2 is a contribution to the debate on next year's plan; taken together the questions imply:

> *'We value your perspective and will take you views into account in the preparation of next year's plan, meanwhile it is you're duty to make the best of whatever resources you have available to you.'*

The integration of review, planning and budgeting can be best achieved through adopting, publishing and working to a planning and reporting cycle. The main events in which are outlined in the example in the next section.

Planning and Reporting Cycle

	Planning	Reporting
August	Market analysis	
Sept	Team review completed	Team review and self-assessment completed; Student achievement known and analyzed
Oct/Nov	(Internal discussions on strategic and operational plans for the forthcoming year)	Quality systems audit; institutional self-assessment
Jan	Draft course programme	Report to Academic Board/ Corporation
Feb	Bids to Funding Council	
Mar	Internal plans/project bids	
Apr	(Discussions on matching operational plans to organizational strategy)	
May	Draft budget planning conference	
June	Draft plans to Academic Board/ Corporation/TEC	
July	Plan published; team review starts	

A System Described

The documentation to support a team review and self-assessment system is included in appendix 2. Some of its main features are outlined below.

The documentation is designed to support a 'one-line' system to be operated by both academic and business support teams emphasizing the importance of improving quality in all parts of the 'quality chain'.

Team review is best carried out within a relatively stable team environment where the individuals concerned feel ownership for the results achieved by the team and the consequences of the actions they plan to take. Course teams can be too narrowly focused for this stability to be achieved, as membership can shift markedly from one year to the next and each individual belongs to a wide range of different teams. In such cases it may be better to define a team structure at a higher level of aggregation, based on groups of staff responsible for a small family of courses on which, by and large they work together. This does not preclude the individuals concerned working for other teams in a servicing arrangement, which then becomes one of the services provided by the team.

The main features of the team review and self-assessment model provided are as follows:

1 Information gathering

This is mainly a team responsibility. Non-prescriptive guidelines allow the team to select relevant information in the light of local circumstances.

2 Information review

Again a checklist to support the discussion is provided. The aim of this section is to promote honest discussion behind closed doors. Any requirement to produce long written reports for management at this stage would, it is argued, reduce the likelihood of this being accomplished. The emphasis throughout is on self-evaluation, self-assessment and action plans.

The framework covers:

- Marketing
- Access guidance and induction (teaching teams only)
- Operation
- Teaching and assessment (teaching teams only)
- Other issues chosen by team members

3 Self-assessment

The approach to be taken in this section was described in chapter 9.

4 Action planning

As issues are identified during the process of review and self-assessment teams are expected to transfer them to the relevant action plan. Reports (and justifications) are not required. The emphasis is very much on: 'If there's a problem what are we going to do about it?'

The action plans are divided in terms of the College aims, with for example, sections on:

- marketing and curriculum
- quality
- staffing
- resources

This format draws attention to the aims and helps both to communicate them through the organization, and encourage teams to respond to them.

The aims on marketing and curriculum are further sub-divided into 'market segments', i.e. groups of students sharing common objectives and other characteristics. In this example school leavers, higher education, employer sponsored day release and adult/community are used.

The use of market segments encourages the teams to look outside themselves and focus on the customer in what otherwise might become a rather closed internal process.

Teams are asked to consider in turn the particular development needs of each group of customer they may come into contact with. In each case the documentation provides a brief labour market summary, again reinforcing the external perspective.

The quality section relates back to the question identified earlier namely:

- What is the best quality we can achieve within the limits of the resources made available to us?

While the second question

- How could resources within the institution be better deployed to enhance quality?

is dealt with separately under the 'resources' aim.

The 'staffing' section separately invites inputs into the staff development and human resource development plans.

An additional section is provided to enable the staff's perception of the quality of internal services provided to be monitored.

Embedding the System

To demonstrate its commitment to the above and other key quality assurance processes senior management will have to:

(i)   check that middle managers are discussing the outcomes of team review with their teams and incorporating useful ideas in their plans where appropriate;

(ii)   check that key quality systems, including team review are being operated effectively by all teams.

Point (i) is relatively easy to accomplish due to the smaller numbers involved. Discussions with the manager concerned or a brief presentation on the actions taken being two possible means of accomplishing this. In large organizations point (ii) will require a more structured approach. The Quality Systems Audit team has proved to be an effective and efficient mechanism in this respect.

The Quality Systems Audit

Quality audit is a well established concept in industry and is gaining hold in education. It can be seen as a relatively low level exercise in which virtually anyone in the organization can be trained as an auditor and as such ask to see a pre-determined checklist of evidence chosen to demonstrate that selected systems and procedures are being operated in accordance with company policy.

An alternative and potentially more powerful approach would be to determine that this 'team' of auditors would be the management team itself. The reasoning behind this being that the attention of the management team will not only underline the organization's commitment to its quality system, but also the expertise and understanding represented will allow the process to assume a development aspect. This in turn will provide for under-performing areas to be given advice and feedback and for the encouragement of improvement.

Such a process could involve:

- a pre-meeting of the team to determine the systems to be audited, the questions to be asked and the evidence required;
- the allocation of all staff teams to an individual auditor;
- a pre-meeting between the auditor and the leaders of his/her allocated teams to explain the process and answer questions where necessary;
- a further meeting with each team leader to review and discuss the availability of evidence requested.

A sample list of questions is included in the team review and self-assessment documentation given in appendix 2, section 5, 'Preparation for Audit'.

A report on this process can be sent to the Scheme Coordinator. A simple scoring system would allow for the publication of an indicator of team performance. Areas where performance is poor can then be taken up with the line manager concerned.

A further meeting of the systems audit team will allow for a review of the audit process and for moderation of the grades emanating from the self-assessment process. This meeting could provide a useful and efficient opportunity for corporation involvement in the institution's quality assurance processes.

The results of this process can be published in the annual report and contribute to the institutional evaluation that it contains.

Institution Level Review

The institution level review, be it in the form of an evaluative college report or self-assessment, is certain to be a key document in any attempt by the organization to demonstrate its approach to quality assurance is sufficiently honest and robust to qualify for a greater degree of independence in its quality assessment arrangements.

The involvement of the governors, in providing an independent oversight of the activities of the institution, will also need to be developed and strengthened in the area of quality assurance.

Two issues will need to be clarified:

(i)   the format for the report and in particular the framework(s) to be adopted;

(ii)   the process by which it is determined and in particular the involvement of the governors.

Report Formats

The optimum time for writing and publishing an evaluative report must be during the autumn term. Figures for:

- volume of student activity
- student achievement
- financial outturns

will become available as will the result of the team review and audit processes where these are in operation.

It is also the ideal time for reflection on the results of the previous year as work begins in earnest on plans for the next.

As part of the evaluation you may consider:

(i)   *Performance against objectives*

Comment on each objective in the Strategic Plan considering;

- objectives achieved;
- objectives not achieved;

- objectives deferred/revised;
- other achievements.

This format carries a number of advantages:

- it reports on progress against the institution's own objectives;
- it gives a comprehensive picture of activity and development over the previous year;
- it strengthens the role of the plan in the operation of the institution.

On the other hand:

- unless the objectives are unusually specific it is usually possible to point to some progress against any objective;
- the report can be rather long and unreadable;
- the emphasis tends to be on success or failure of existing plans rather than possible new directions.

(ii) *Evaluation against a quality framework*

A realistic evaluation of strengths and weaknesses against a selected quality framework can be a revealing exercise. All the more so if it links with the self-assessment process described earlier and builds into a full institutional review. The report would consist of a list of strengths and weaknesses against each of the elements of the framework examples of which have been fully described in chapters 2, 3 and 4. English further education colleges are in any case required to produce such a report to support the inspection process using the 'Assessing Achievement' framework described earlier.

The final report can be pulled together by a team of senior managers informed by a middle management conference to make the link with team review.

Focus groups can concentrate on elements of the framework (for example, responsiveness and range, teaching and the promotion of learning etc. in the case of assessing achievement) before meeting to agree the main features of the report.

Scoring and grading systems can be introduced as this stage using FEFC definitions (see chapter 1) based on the balance of strengths and weaknesses or the systems described in models such as the Malcolm Baldridge Awards and the European Foundation for Quality Management and the British Quality Foundation (chapter 3).

This approach has the potential to:

- meet the requirements of funding bodies;
- strengthen self-assessment;

- suggest new areas for development;
- provide a readable overview of activity;
- expose weaknesses as well as strengths.

It will not, however:

- give prominence to your own objectives;
- emphasize the role of the Strategic Plan.

It will also only be as comprehensive and valid as the framework you have selected.

(iii) *Following up outcomes*

In most cases the longest established quality assurance mechanism in education has been the analysis and following up of examination success rates. This process has been supplemented in recent years by other data such as completion rates, student destinations and value added scores. I have argued earlier that statistical considerations make it unreasonable for an individual teacher to be held accountable for one year's results taken in isolation. There are too many variables outside the control of any individual. As the sample size increases, however, either by examining averages over time or aggregate scores over larger numbers of students (for example, at department or College level) the statistical validity of the data increases.

A format for collection of data on examination success could be as follows:

Course	Number enrolled	Number completed	Percentage pass	Percentage pass average last three years	National average	Team target
1						
2						
3 etc.						
Section average						

In some circumstances value added scores and/or grade profile will be appropriate.

Where there are areas of concern these should be the subject of an action plan where possible as part of team review.

An audit process to check that the system was being operated and identify areas where management action is necessary could involve review by a senior manager or public reporting processes, for example to the Academic Board.

Governors' Involvement

As the implications of incorporation have gradually been revealed the role of the governing body has gradually changed. From its initial emphasis on finance and resources followed rapidly by an involvement in personnel issues emphasized in further education by the long-running contracts dispute, the third age of incorporation could well be an involvement in quality assurance. After a slow start the main impetus for this is coming from the Inspectorate who now see part of their role in encouraging self-assessment as an important driver for quality improvement and see the interest and attention of the corporation in such matters as an indispensable ingredient. In further education the governors' role has two main themes:

- supporting the College:

    — promoting the College's interests;
    — fostering good relationships;
    — offering constructive criticism;
    — communicating with local business.

- Oversight of the College's activities:

    — ensuring oversight of how the Principal carries out management responsibilities;
    — not becoming involved in detailed scrutiny of management, administration and teaching programmes;
    — providing a clear framework of accountability;
    — agreeing policies and strategies to enable progress to be monitored;
    — having the means of knowing whether the College is properly managed.

The *FEFC Guide for Governors* also directs that the Board will need to determine:

- the areas of performance it needs to monitor;
- the appropriate performance indicators;
- the management information required.

The amount of time that corporation members will be willing or able to put into this activity is necessarily limited. The key to effective governors involvement lies in establishing an agreed framework of policy, indicators and reports which provide an adequate, reliable and efficient indication of the health and development of the institution. In respect of quality assurance the elements of this framework have been outlined in earlier chapters. The most important of these being:

- the College quality policy;
- the performance indicators strategy
- the College report (in particular the evaluation of strengths and weaknesses against the established quality framework).

Chapter 13

Assuring Quality in Franchising

With the publication of FEFC *Circular 96/06* the franchising of College provision into third party providers has been confirmed as a legitimate activity, if it is undertaken within the strict criteria described. Similar arrangements are possible in Scotland and Wales, although the rules vary.

In many cases these arrangements have involved colleges in responsibility for the delivery of large volumes of training, often in remote locations, using staff not directly employed by the College.

In such circumstances the operation of an effective quality assurance system must be a major concern. The systems audit approach described throughout this publication, provides both an efficient and hopefully effective mechanism for achieving this.

The following should be present:

- a franchising policy, approved by the corporation;
- an approvals mechanism, independent of those involved in sales and marketing whose conclusions are reported to the Board;
- a quality handbook, outlining the requirements and procedures to be undertaken by franchisees;
- a quality audit process, to identify and report on the analogue of key College quality systems operated by the franchisee.

The quality audit should be undertaken by a member of the College staff assigned to the franchisee and include reference to the following:

Quality criteria	Evidence of achievement	Action/comment
Does the franchisee have a policy on quality?		
Is the franchisee committed to an externally recognized quality standard?		
Will the college teaching and learning standards be achieved?		
What is the franchisee doing to close any gap between the current success rate and their target success rate?		

Quality criteria	Evidence of achievement	Action/comment
Will the learners be properly inducted into the learning programme?		
Will the programme be delivered by suitably qualified trainers in a safe learning environment?		
Will the deliverers require any further support and training?		
Will the learners have access to adequate learning resources?		
Will the learners be assigned to a personal tutor/mentor for individual support and guidance throughout their programme?		
Are the necessary procedures in place for the effective monitoring, evaluation and review of the training and the learning which includes feedback from the learner?		
Is there an effective procedure for internal verification of NVQs of consistent and effective procedures for other training programmes?		
Are the systems for the gathering, processing and storage of information and data adequate to meet the obligations stated in the contract?		

It is important that the outcomes of this process should be passed through the College's regular quality assurance arrangements, with issues receiving similar treatment, say, to the reports provided by external verifiers. They should also be considered by the independent review committee before contracts are signed and reviewed. The requirements of this audit process should be contractual to allow the organization to withdraw from agreements where quality is shown to be inadequate.

Conclusions and Issues

This book has set out provide a number of ideas and suggestions. You may choose to use adapt or reject them. In doing so you will develop ideas of your own as you investigate one of the most complex managerial issues known, the improvement of quality in education. Throughout the book there has been a number of recurring themes some of which I bring together, by way of a conclusion:

- decide what quality means for you in line with the overall strategy of the organization;
- quality in education will not improve unless the staff of the organization are motivated to do so. Keep this in mind when you develop new systems;
- team development and empowerment will help and provide staff with the necessary authority to make changes;
- the attitudes and attention of management is crucial.

Appendix 1

Course Design Standards

The following checklist can be used by the course team, or those involved in the process of course approvals, to determine an appropriate set of standards for a given course or programme area.

1 MARKETING

QUALITY CHARACTERISTIC	PROBE QUESTION	ACCEPTABLE EVIDENCE	STANDARDS
Market awareness	How did you/have you/will you determine that (i) there is a market (ii) the extent of that market?	Questionnaire — analyses statistics — qualitative data, (letters, requests). Statistics — numerical data.	
Advertising	How did you/have you/will you advertise the course?		
Advertising course marketing material	Is the existing course publicity material enough to meet your requirements? If yes — what material/ media do you employ? If not — what is required to improve your marketing?	Full courses!	
Marketing/ advertising costs	Are the present methods of marketing cost effective? How have you measured this? Is there any other method which you think would improve the cost effectiveness?	Numerical data. Discussion document?	
Marketing effectiveness	Is your present advertising/ marketing effective? How have you defined this efficiency? If not effective how do you envisage improving the efficiency?	Yes/no Statistical — data Discussion document?	
Marketing responsibility	Who markets the course? Who would you like to market the course? If not present marketer why do you want to change?		

2 COURSE DESIGN

QUALITY CHARACTERISTIC	PROBE QUESTION	ACCEPTABLE EVIDENCE	STANDARDS
Mode of attendance	What modes are offered? Is this sufficient to meet the market needs? If not sufficient what plans do you have to rectify this?	Prospectus Questionnaires? Advisory board review minutes Course team minutes	
Course leader	What qualifications does the course leader require? How did you decide on these requirements? Does the CL meet all these requirements? If not, what plans are there to correct any shortcomings?	BTEC requirements Course review documents Management reviews Personal achievement record	
Course team	Who comprises the course team? How was the composition of the course teamdecided? What are the qualifications/skills of the people on the course team? Do the members of the course team meet all the requirements to fulfil their roles? What needs to be/or has been/done to ensure that the team members are equipped to meet their obligations? How frequently does the course team meet? If the team does not include all lecturers involved in delivering the course how are the non-members kept informed?	Training records Personal assessments Personal achievement records Team meeting minutes Team meeting minutes Example of communication	
Course format	What subjects are included in this course? How was the decision to include these subjects taken?	Course programme BTEC requirement Review document	

QUALITY CHARACTERISTIC	PROBE QUESTION	ACCEPTABLE EVIDENCE	STANDARDS
	Do these subjects satisfy the requirements for progression to a more advanced course? If not what are the students advised to do next?	BTEC requirement	
	Have you considered the possibility of changing the course content to encourage progression where feasible? Are there any compulsory units?	Course review Minutes or section heads review	
	Are any of these core units which could be integrated with other courses in this faculty of other faculties? Have you considered combining these where low numbers would indicate it to be feasible/desirable? Are any of the units offered optional?	BTEC submission	
	Are there options dictated by numbers? Are the options dictated by availability of staff?	BTEC submission	
	Are any options dictated by the client(s)? Are any of the options suitable for combined classes?	Team minutes	
	Have you collected or been provided with any evidence that the course meets the customers requirements?	Feedback from employers Questionnaires Analysis of advanced course results	

3 ACCESS AND INDUCTION

QUALITY CHARACTERISTIC	PROBE QUESTION	ACCEPTABLE EVIDENCE	STANDARDS
Entry criteria	Do you have formal entry criteria? Do you have informal entry criteria? Where are they stated? What flexibility is there?	Student enrolment form/Record of Achievement Interview information and records.	
	Are there artificial barriers to entry?	Statistical records of students.	
Equal opportunities	Is the publicity and advertising unbiased?	In prospectus and course leaflets and placed in the schools/youth clubs/library community centres and shops.	
	Is unbiased guidance and counselling provided?	Marketing materials/previous comments made by tutors/did they have Record of Achievement (ROA) or equivalent?	
	Which modes of attendance and methods of delivery do you employ?	Full/PT/flexible/open/distance modular.	
	Are all applicants interviewed?	Interviewing schedules.	
	Where are they interviewed?	Suitable room.	
	Are costs a barrier?	If information in the prospectus	
	What financial support is available?	Where there is a need students are referred to Student Services.	
	How do you ensure you meet the needs of all students?	Presence of disabled student. Ethnic groups, specific learning difficulties.	

QUALITY CHARACTERISTIC	PROBE QUESTION	ACCEPTABLE EVIDENCE	STANDARDS
	What support internal or external do you offer them?	Existence of support staff/agencies to where students have been referred.	
APL	What recognition is given for relevant prior learning?	APL Policy Statement. Documents which record. Trained assessors are available. Student portfolios including APL.	
Induction Policy and Practice	Do you have an induction policy?	Documents/induction. Plan/student handbooks. Are outcomes communicated to students?	
	How is this carried out?	Is a period of time allocated. Participants involved/ plan of time period.	
	How is it assessed for effectiveness?	Student retention. Career path decisions.	
	Do you ask student opinions?	Level of motivation/ ability to learn, students evaluation of induction.	
	How close is the induction to course programme outcomes?	Students can identify the link between induction and the performance in the evaluation.	

4 COURSE OPERATION

QUALITY CHARACTERISTIC	PROBE QUESTION	EXAMPLES OF ACCEPTABLE EVIDENCE	STANDARDS
Team operations	How often do the course team meet?	Records of meetings	
	How formal are meetings?	Minutes and agenda published and distributed effectively.	
	What % of course team attends each meeting?	All team members, including P/T are regularly involved.	
	How is attendance safeguarded?	Proactive timing/ timetables/diary entries before start of course.	
	What issues are covered?	Over time, should cover full range	
Course design and timetable	What is overall structure of course? e.g. modular, linear?	Logical structure, whatever the model.	
	Can students join/leave at various points?	Provision, where appropriate, for flexible entry.	
	When is timetable published? to whom?	At beginning of course, for all members, subject to renegotiation.	
	What provision is there in course design for negotiating the curriculum?	Space in programme for monitoring changing needs and renegotiating programme as necessary.	
	What are work experience arrangements? What preparation/feedback is given?	Reports from students re 'added value' perceptions from work experience.	
Adherence to programme objectives and specified learning outcomes	How do you ensure that the programme adheres to published objectives and learning outcomes?	Regular inspections of students/ staff work books. PDP reports.	

QUALITY CHARACTERISTIC	PROBE QUESTION	EXAMPLES OF ACCEPTABLE EVIDENCE	STANDARDS
Vocational relevance	What mechanisms are deployed to ensure the programme is vocationally relevant?	Student learning experiences and practical work is vocationally relevant. Realistic work environments are available to students.	
	What provision is made for employer liaison?	Evidence of employer consultation with the management and delivery of the programme.	
	What arrangements are made for work experience and simulation?	Systems for management and assessment of students whilst on work placement. Valid simulation opportunities.	
Appropriate teaching methods	What range of teaching methods is used?	The methods should be appropriate to identified student needs / stated outcomes.	
	Are the teaching and learning strategies open to negotiation between staff and students?	Schemes of work/ lesson plans	
	Do the teaching and learning strategies integrate core-skills / work experience into the learning process?	Lesson plans / schemes of work	
Tutoring	How are personal tutors allocated? What tutorial programme is operated?	Records of group and individual tutorials.	

QUALITY CHARACTERISTIC	PROBE QUESTION	EXAMPLES OF ACCEPTABLE EVIDENCE	STANDARDS
	How do students access general facilities / non-course-related activities?	Information given to new students refacilities / counselling / who's who / calendar of events / counselling service plus reports on take-up.	
	What careers guidance is given?	Reports on use of careers service / careers library etc.	
Student records	How do you monitor student attainment and development?	Appropriate proformas are produced and kept up to date. Feedback on progress is provided to students Action plans are negotiated as a result of formative assessment.	
Quality control procedures	What arrangements do you operate for course review?	Formative evaluation during course involving students. End of course review documentation to include feedback from students exam results. Action plans resulting from review. Changes made to implement action plans. Moderator's report.	

5 RESOURCES

QUALITY CHARACTERISTIC	PROBE QUESTION	ACCEPTABLE EVIDENCE	STANDARDS
Teaching staff	What are the full time and part time class contact hours?	Asking FT and PT course team staff. Information from MIS and Div. Manager.	
Industrial experience	What are your relevant industrial experiences, relevant qualifications?	CVs ask course tutor, check College records.	
	Is your assessment experience adequate for the course needs?	See historical records Employer's and student comments.	
Commitment		Response to questions, look straight in the eye. Student's notes and records. Marketing scheme.	
Support	Are you receiving adequate teaching support?	Observations of workplace. Attitude to students in data collection, standards of work, material presentation.	
Equipment	Observations on equipment by yourselves.	Asking students, review of same.	

6 ASSESSMENT AND OUTCOMES

QUALITY CHARACTERISTIC	PROBE QUESTION	ACCEPTABLE EVIDENCE	STANDARDS
Assignment strategies	What are the assessment methods?	Competence list or phase tests/ assignments or coursework or internal exams or external exams or RoA (some or all)	
	Can you provide this year's results for the above?	Lists	
	How do you compare with previous years?	Lists	
	How do you ensure consistency of standards and comparability with other establishments?	National pass rates Moderators' reports	
	What enrichment experiences do the students get and are they accredited?		
	Have you compared entry and exit qualifications?		
Student reports	What reports do students receive during and at the end of the course?	Documentary evidence.	
	Other academic feedback to students during the course?	Documentary evidence.	
	What reports are made to employers? When and how frequent?	Documentary evidence.	

QUALITY CHARACTERISTIC	PROBE QUESTION	ACCEPTABLE EVIDENCE	STANDARDS
	How detailed are the reports?	Documentary evidence.	
	Do you get feedback from students?	Questionnaire.	
	Do they have representative members of the course team?	Documentary evidence of course team reports.	
	For FT under-18 students, do you see parents to discuss progress?		

The above standards were devised by Margaret Hawksley and the Swindon College Curriculum Consultants.

Team Review and Self-assessment

Sample Documentation

CONTENTS

Mission and introduction
Information gathering
Information review and self-assessment
Action planning
 Marketing and curriculum
 Quality
 Staffing
 Resources
Comment on College services

Introduction

Our Mission

> 'Our mission is to provide ...'

Our Aim

To work for **continuous improvement** in the standards of the courses and services we provide responding to the needs of our students, and our internal and external customers.

In pursuit of this staff will be expected to:

    (i)   work cooperatively in teams;

    (ii)   reflect on the operation of, and outcomes from, courses and services for which they are responsible;

    (iii)   define realistically the total resources they require for operation and development;

    (iv)   make the best possible use of whatever resources are made available to them.

College management will be expected to:

    (i)   consider the views of staff teams in drawing up College plans and operating proposals;

    (ii)   delegate operational control to the lowest practical level;

    (iii)   monitor the effectiveness of the operation of the College and its systems;

    (iv)   provide support to staff in the implementation of College plans.

Each team reviews its course or service at the end of the academic year. Guidelines to assist in this process are attached.

Information Gathering

The team leader will be responsible for gathering information and presenting it to the team for their consideration and comment.

    Possible sources of relevant information include:

Teaching teams

Exam results analysis (current year)
No of students enrolled
No of students completed

Student retention
Student feedback/customer satisfaction surveys
Moderator reports
Inspection reports
Published national averages
Course submission/validation documentation
Destination analysis
Budget proposals
Previous year's action plans
Inspection reports and feedback

Service teams

List of main internal and external customer groups
Customer satisfaction surveys
Directorate budget proposals
Previous year's action plans
Inspection reports and feedback

You will find the following documents useful in this process:

The College Charter
The College Strategic Plan (or Summary)
The College teaching standards

Information Review and Self-assessment

The team is meeting to discuss what can be done to improve the quality of the course or service offered and what *could* be done in future with realistic levels of support from the College.

The following definition has been adopted by the College:

'Quality is defined...'

The 'customer' can be *external* (for example, students or employers) or *internal* to the College (for example, lecturers using the print room etc.).

Review

The following checklist has been drawn up to aid discussions for both teams involved in teaching and the provision of College services.

Some sections are applicable to both teaching and service teams, others to teaching teams only (as indicated).

(i) *Marketing (teaching and service teams)*
     Who are the customers for this course/service?
     Does the course/service meet customer needs?
     What are its aims?
     Do we know what our customers think about it?
     Is there a demand for it?
     Is the publicity/promotion/information adequate?

(ii) *Access guidance and Induction (teaching teams)*
      Are the entry criteria relevant?
      Is the ethnic/gender/age balance right?
      Is there a clear induction process?
      Is there provision for special needs?

(iii) *Operation (teaching and service teams)*
       Does the team operate effectively?
       Are resources used to their best advantage? (people, time, materials, equipment and premises)
       Are the materials used appropriate?
       Do we discuss the quality of teaching/services with students/customers?
       Is the administration of record keeping effective?

(iv) *Teaching and assessment (teaching teams)*
      Are the teaching and learning strategies appropriate?
      Are the assessment and assignment strategies appropriate?
      What is the success rate/retention rate/post-course destination?
      Are library/learning support facilities adequate?

(v) *Other issues chosen by team members*

Self-assessment

- College quality policy implies that quality is more likely to improve where staff teams accept responsibility for quality improvement.
- The FEFC is making it clear that the next round of inspections will be very different from the first.
- Colleges which have a robust and credible self-assessment procedure can look forward to a lighter touch in future without the intrusion and disruption which inevitably characterizes a full scale inspection.

The process

1   Team leaders will meet with a member of the College Quality Audit Team to explain the process and outline the audit evidence to be provided.

2   Staff will complete a confidential 'individual self-assessment' in advance of meeting as a team.

3   Teams will meet to complete the team review and self-assessment process using the documentation attached.
    Members of other teams should be invited to participate.

4   Teams will assess their performance against a range of criteria using FEFC definitions, namely:

> Grade 1 — provision which has many strengths and very few weaknesses
>
> Grade 2 — provision in which the strengths clearly outweigh the weaknesses
>
> Grade 3 — provision with a balance of strengths and weaknesses
>
> Grade 4 — provision in which the weaknesses clearly outweigh the strengths
>
> Grade 5 — provision which has many weaknesses and very few strengths

5   Action to deal with weaknesses and develop strengths should be transferred to the relevant Action Plan (Forms 1–7).

6   Teams will meet with their line manager to agree the self-assessment grade awarded and work through the action plan and its implications.

7   Members of the Quality Audit Team will meet with line managers to discuss the self-assessment grade awarded.

8   Members of the Quality Audit Team will meet team leaders to collect audit evidence, including evidence for the grade agreed.

9   Members of the Quality Audit Team will meet, with members of the Corporation in attendance, to agree grading policy and issues raised during the audit process.

10 The self-assessment grade will be published as part of the College report.

Increasing Effectiveness: A Guide to Quality Management

Self-assessment
Form (i)   Quality of Teaching and Learning (Teaching Teams only)

Quality Indicators (*derived from College teaching standards*)	Grade 1–5	Evidence
1 Course programme		
A course programme for staff and students is published which includes:		
arrangements for induction and initial assessment		
course timetable and calendar		
assessment programme and deadlines		
progression details		
2 Teaching/learning		
aims and objectives are clearly stated		
learning support is provided at the appropriate level for each student		
the programme is delivered effectively using a range of teaching and learning strategies		
the resources used are appropriate		
each student has a termly review and action plan		
class and course surveys are conducted and responded to		
personal contact is made with absentees		

3 Tutoring		
a tutorial programme is prepared and published to the student		
the programme is delivered consistently with a mix of individual and group sessions		
each student is helped to work on and complete a personal development plan		

GRADE THIS SECTION	

Weaknesses identified should be transferred to the relevant action plan.

Self-assessment
Form (ii)   Quality of Other Services

Quality indicators	Grade 1–5	Evidence
Services to external customers/students (please list).		
Services to internal customers/ College staff (please list).		

GRADE THIS SECTION	

Weaknesses identified should be transferred to the relevant action plan.

Self-assessment
Form (iii)   Staff Skills and Team Work

Quality indicators	Grade 1–5	Evidence
The overall balance of skills within the team is appropriate to the work undertaken.		
The effectiveness of individuals within the team in delivering the courses/services provided.		
Regular effective team meetings are held.		
Members are involved in decision making.		
Team communications between members of the team and other teams are good. Briefing sessions are held and attended.		
The team plans development, quality improvement and effective use of resources.		
Team sets and meets standards and targets.		

GRADE THIS SECTION	

Weaknesses identified should be transferred to the relevant action plan.

Self-assessment
Form (iv)   Outcomes

Quality indicators	Grade 1–5	Evidence
Exam results are good compared with relevant national averages.		
Retention rates are good.		
Progression to relevant employment/further study is documented and at a high level.		
Customer satisfaction is documented and at a high level.		
Student numbers are increasing (where applicable).		
Budget management is good (where applicable).		
Service standards are achieved.		
Other outcomes (please specify).		

GRADE THIS SECTION	

Weaknesses identified should be transferred to the relevant action plan.

Self-assessment
Form (v)   The Operation of College Procedures

Quality Indicators	Grade 1–5	Evidence
1 A list of team members and courses/services is provided.		
2 A copy of the team review action plan for 1994–95 and evidence of successful follow up is available.		
3 Team review action plans for 1995–96 with relevant information completed (section 3).		
4 There is evidence of regular team activity for example, a 'team log' accessible to all team members containing minutes of meetings, feedback documentation, schedules, etc.		
5 A comprehensive calendar of team meetings for the 1996–97 session has been produced and published.		
6 Feedback from students (all courses) or a sample of customers (services) is obtained. (for example, completed customer satisfaction/survey forms/action plans).		
7 College internal verification procedures are being followed on all NVQ/GNVQ courses offered.		
8 Evidence that early leaver procedures have been followed through by course tutors and class registers have been completed satisfactorily is available.		

GRADE THIS SECTION	

Weaknesses identified should be transferred to the relevant action plan.

SELF-ASSESSMENT SUMMARY

_____ TEAM

	Grade 1–5	
(i) Quality of teaching and learning		
(ii) Quality of other services		
(iii) Staff skills and team work		
(iv) Outcomes		
(v) Operation of College procedures		

OVERALL GRADE	

Signed _____ Team Leader   Agreed by _____ Line Manager

Action Planning — Team response to College aims

The College aims have been used as a framework to structure the College plan. You should also refer to Divisional/Unit and Faculty/Directorate plans where available.

Please use the forms provided to identify the contribution the team will make to achieving these aims. You may also use the space to comment on contributions you would like to see from other parts of the organization or to suggest changes in the aims themselves.

This feedback will be discussed at a senior management team conference during the autumn term.

- Specific, Measurable, Achievable TARGETS and STANDARDS should be set wherever possible.
- RESPONSIBILITY should normally be allocated to a named member of the team.

Copies of the forms should be returned to your line manager **no later than** ... and each time it is updated.

College Aims — Marketing and Curriculum

(College aims can be listed here to increase their prominence and encourage a response from staff)

The College response is structured by looking at the need of different client groups ('market segments'). In each case some basic information on labour market trends for each group is included to help focus the discussion.

FORM 1

ACTION PLAN 1 — **DEVELOPMENTS PROPOSED FOR SEGMENT . . .**
repeated for all segments

TEAM   TEAM LEADER

PLANNED DEVELOPMENT	RESPONSIBILITY	RESOURCES ALLOCATED	QUALITY TARGET*

* Wherever possible TARGETS should be SMART — specific, measurable, achievable, realistic and time constrained.
A copy of this form should be returned to the line manager by . . . and circulated to all team members.

College Aim — Quality

(List relevant aims here)

List the improvements you plan to make paying special attention to:

- Action on areas which fell below targets/standards/expectation.
- Action to improve equality of opportunities for existing/potential customers/students.
- Action to address issues raised during the recent FEFC inspection.
- Action to address issues raised in your own self assessment.

Team response — use Form 2

FORM 2

ACTION PLAN 2 — **DEVELOPMENTS PLANNED TO IMPROVE QUALITY WITHIN EXISTING RESOURCES**

TEAM   TEAM LEADER

PLANNED DEVELOPMENT	RESPONSIBILITY	RESOURCES ALLOCATED	QUALITY TARGET

A copy of this form should be returned to the line manager by . . . and circulated to all team members

College Aims — Staffing

(List relevant aims here)

In addition to any general comments the team should consider the staff development support its members will need to carry through the changes planned.

Team response — use Form 3.

FORM 3 — **WHAT STAFF CHANGES/DEVELOPMENT DO YOU NEED TO HELP ACHIEVE YOUR OBJECTIVES?**

STAFF DEVELOPMENT REQUIREMENTS FOR THE FORTHCOMING YEAR

TEAM   TEAM LEADER

PLANNED DEVELOPMENT (FROM FORMS 1 AND 2)	STAFF CHANGES/ DEVELOPMENT	INDIVIDUAL NAME/TEAM

A copy of this form should be returned to your line manager by . . . and circulated to all team members.

College Aims — Resources

(List College aims here)

You should include your proposals for the following:

- apparatus and equipment (including large 'capital' items).
- changes in the pattern of consumables required.
- books and periodicals (including library stock).
- premises requirements.

Please be realistic in your requests as the College has limited resources at its disposal. Major development projects should be discussed with your line manager before significant development work is undertaken.

Team response — use Form 4.

FORM 4

ACTION PLAN 4 — **PROJECTS PROPOSED FOR NEXT YEAR'S BUDGET**

TEAM   TEAM LEADER

PLANNED DEVELOPMENT	RESPONSIBILITY	RESOURCES REQUIRED	QUALITY TARGET

A copy of this form should be returned to the line manager by . . . and circulated to all team members.

4 Comment on College Services

As an internal customer of College services we welcome the views of the team on the quality of the services provided.

Please record your considered team view on form 5 and return this direct to the Quality Manager no later than. . . .

The result will complement the information gained by teams as part of their own customer satisfaction surveys.

FORM 5

FROM _____ TEAM

How satisfied is the team with the following College services?

	Very			Not at all
Counselling, welfare and pastoral support				
Customer services				
Finance				
Office services				
Learning resources				
Information services				
Management services (CMT)				
Management services (Faculty/Directorate)				
Marketing				
Personnel				
Premises				
Refectory services				
Staff development				

Other comments

The College aims and strategies are set out in the Strategic Plan (or an Executive Summary, if available)
What changes (if any) would you like to see in these in future?

Appendix 3

Customer Satisfaction Surveys

A sample set of 'customer satisfaction' survey forms is included in the appendix. The forms provide a compromise between the highly structured models already widely used throughout education and the unstructured model, described in the text, which leaves the choice of issue to the customer. The model described here provides some structure, which was appreciated by students who found the write-in sections rather onerous, combined with the option to customize.

Most of the forms contain the following:

Part 1 — set by central college.
Part 2 — set by the individual member of staff or team (if required).
Part 3 — a space for optional comment by the student or internal customer.

Divisions/units may substitute their own model (subject to approval).

The main features are as follows:

1 Class Survey

All teachers are required to consult with the students on their perceptions of the class during the first term. This can be done verbally if preferred but a note of actions agreed must be kept. The form is available for use if preferred.

2 Course Survey

Distributed by all course tutors at the end of the first term.
Report to the immediate line manager.
Line managers return the 'overall opinion' to the manager responsible for quality using the response form provided.

3 Service Survey

To be distributed by all service unit managers to a sample of customers during the academic year.
Unit managers return the 'overall opinion' to the Manager responsible for quality using the response form provided.

4 Faculty/Directorate Management Survey

For circulation by management teams.
A similar form can be used by the senior management team

5 Response Form

As outlined in 2 and 3 above.
Other sample surveys can be undertaken on specific issues, for example, induction; enrolment; tutorial arrangements etc.

6 Leavers Form

To complete the system a leavers form can be circulated directly to all student leaving a course, either early or on completion of the course. Broad questions such as 'Were you satisfied with the course?', 'Would you recommend this course to a friend?' or 'Did the course fulfil your expectations?', can provide a useful central check on the effectiveness of this highly delegated system. Areas where there is cause for concern can then be investigated in more detail.

Customer Satisfaction Survey

Class Survey Form	Class:	Lecturer:

Please take a few minutes to give me your opinion on the points listed below. It will help me in planning the remainder of the course.

Key: 1 Excellent — 5 Poor: please tick one box

Part 1	1	2	3	4	5
Information about the class and its aims					
The content of the class					
The teaching and support from the lecturer					
The organization of the class					
The materials, equipment and facilities used					
The amount covered in each lecture					
The marking of assignments, homework etc.					

Part 2 — Questions the lecturer may wish to add

Part 3 (optional) — Please use this space for things you would like to comment on

Guidelines

- The use of this form is now optional. Lecturers *must* however consult with the students on their options on the class approximately half-way through the first term and keep a note of any agreed actions.
- This form can be circulated by any class teacher whenever it would be useful to do so.
- The survey is designed to encourage feedback from students at an early stage in the expectation of corrective action being taken where possible.
- The results need not be shared with the course team or College managers unless you wish to.
- Part 2 enables you to add your own questions if you wish.
- The results of the survey should be discussed with the students.
- The forms should be kept on file for at least one year to provide evidence that the procedure has been carried out.
- You may substitute a form/procedure of your own design if you wish, provided it covers the points listed over and you are able to supply evidence of it having been used.

Customer Satisfaction Survey

Course Survey Form	Course:	Tutor:

Please take a few minutes to give me your opinion on the points listed below. It will help me in planning the remainder of the course.

Key: 1 Excellent — 5 Poor please tick one box

Part 1	1	2	3	4	5
Information about the course and its aims					
The support from the course tutor					
The organization of the course					
The materials, equipment and facilities used					
Your overall opinion of the class/module					
Your overall opinion of the class/module					
Your overall opinion of the class/module					
Your overall opinion of the class/module					
Your overall opinion of the class/module					
Your overall opinion of the class/module					
Your overall opinion of the course to date					

Part 2 — Questions from the course team

Part 3 (optional) — Please use this space for things you would like to comment on

Guidelines for staff

- This form should be circulated by each course tutor to every course at the end of the first term.
- The survey is designed to encourage feedback from students at an early stage in the expectation of corrective action being taken where possible.
- Please write the names of specific modules/classes in part 1.
- The results must be shared with the course team joined, where possible, by student representatives and communicated to the line manager together with suggestions for action.
- *The results of the question on 'overall opinion of the course to date' should be collated by the Line Manager and passed to the Quality Manager by the end of the spring term.*
- Part 2 enables you to add your own questions if you wish.
- The results of the survey should be discussed with the students.
- The forms should be kept on file for at least one year to provide evidence that the procedure has been carried out.
- You may substitute a form/procedure of your own design if you wish, subject to the approval of the Quality Manager.
- Low scores on individual modules should be followed up, for example, by using the class survey form.

Customer Satisfaction Survey

Service Survey Form	Service:	Team Leader/Manager:

Please take a few minutes to give me your opinion on the points listed below. It will help me in planning the remainder of the course.

Key: 1 Excellent — 5 Poor: please tick one box

Part 1	1	2	3	4	5
The responsiveness of the team					
The effectiveness of the service we provide					
The range and scope of the services provided					
The approachability of team members					
The availability of the service					
Your overall opinion of the service provided					

Part 2 — Questions from the team

Part 3 (optional) — Please use this space for things you would like to comment on

Guidelines for staff

- This form should be circulated by each service team leader to a representative sample of your customers some time during the college year.
- The results should be discussed by the team and used as a basis for planning improvements to the services they provide.
- You may wish to ask for comment on specific feature of the services you provide in section 2.
- *The results of the question on 'overall opinion of the service' should be passed to the Quality Manager by the end of the summer term.*
- The forms should be kept on file for at least one year to provide evidence that the procedure has been carried out.
- You may substitute a form/procedure of your own design if you wish, subject to the approval of the Quality Manager.

Customer Satisfaction Survey

Management Team Survey	Team:	Manager:

Please let us have your opinion of the management services provided by the Management Team. We will use this information in our team review and evaluation.

Key: 1 Excellent — 5 Poor: please tick one box

	1	2	3	4	5
Our effectiveness communicating the College mission, aims and strategy					
Our effectiveness at managing the day-to-day operation					
Our ability to communicate					
Our ability to motivate the staff					
Our responsiveness to requests from staff					
Our availability to meet and talk with staff when required					
Our visibility around the College					
Our effectiveness at managing the resources available					

Faculty/Directorate questions

Increasing Effectiveness: A Guide to Quality Management

Please add any comment your may wish to make (optional)

Please tick as appropriate

TEACHING		TECHNICIAN		ADMIN.		OTHER SUPPORT		FULL TIME		PART TIME	

Customer Satisfaction Survey

Line Manager's Response Form	Unit/Division:	Manager:

Please return the results of the question on **'your overall opinion of the course/service'** for each of the courses/services which have been surveyed. This form should be returned to the Quality Manager by the end of the Spring term (courses) and the end of the summer term (services).

No of responses with score

Course/service surveyed	1	2	3	4	5

Part-time Staff Appraisal

Undertaking appraisal for part-time hourly paid lecturing staff, who may only work for the College for a relatively short time, or only a few hours a week, can present a considerable challenge.

Some colleges have responded by introducing a minimum hours limit to indicate which of their staff qualify for inclusion in the appraisal process.

For colleges where large numbers of such staff are employed, however, not only does the problem become more difficult to manage, but also the cumulative contribution to the quality of delivery becomes more significant.

In such circumstances a 'checklist on entry' can be devised as part of the contracting process. The checklist is used to structure the process of agreement between the part timer and the member of the college staff who is making the arrangements. College staff would normally receive training for this purpose to ensure compliance with College procedures and sufficient knowledge of legislative requirements in this area.

The checklist should include the following:

- Do you know which team you will be working with?
- Who is your contact/mentor within the team?
- Do you know where to find your desk/pigeon hole/work room/ telephone no?
- Are you a trained teacher?
- Do you have a copy of the syllabus/scheme of work for what you are required to teach?
- Do you feel competent to undertake every aspect of this?
- Will you be involved in assessment/internal verification?
- Have you the necessary TDLB awards?
- Are you aware of where you can get support for:
    — the subject material
    — course delivery issues
    — course materials and administration?

In areas where problems are unearthed appropriate information or support can be offered either 'on the spot' or by referral within the College, for example to the Staff Development Unit.

Completion of this checklist should be checked by administration before a contract is issued.

References

CROSBY, P.B. (1978) *Quality is Free*, New York, McGraw Hill.

DEMING, W.E. (1986) *Out of the Crisis*, Cambridge, MA, MIT Centre for Advanced Engineering Study.

FEFC (1994) *Measuring Achievement* (Circular 94/12), November, London, FEFC.

FEFC (1996) *Achievements of Colleges on their Charter Commitments*, January, London, FEFC.

MILLER, J. and INNISS, S. (1992) *Strategic Quality Management — A Guide for Analysing the Process*, Ware, Hartfordshire, Consultants at Work.

SALLIS, E. and HINGLEY, P. *et al.* (1992) 'Total quality management', *Coombe Lodge Report*, **23**, 1.

Other Reading

AMSDEN, D., BUTLER, H. and AMSDEN, R. (1991) *SPC Simplified for Services*, London, Chapman and Hall.

AVON QUALITY STRATEGIES UNIT (1991) *Defining Quality (Quality Strategy Paper No 3)*, Bristol, Avon Quality Strategies Unit.

BSI QUALITY ASSURANCE (1991) *BS5750: Guidance Notes for Application to Education and Training*, BSI.

CASTLE, J.A. (1992) *Integrated Quality System, or IQS — A TQ Model Based on Systems Perspectives*, Bristol.

CHASE, R. (Ed) (1992) *Managing Service Quality*, ???, IFS Publications.

CHECKLAND, P. (1981) *Systems Thinking, Systems Practice*, Chichester, John Wiley.

CREELAN, E.J. (1993 'Empowerment, TQM', *Magazine*, June, MCB University Press.

DEPARTMENT FOR EDUCATION (DFE) (1993) *The Charter for Further Education*, London, DFE.

DES (1991) *Quality Assurance in Colleges of Further Education — A Report by HMI (92/92/NS)*, London, HMSO.

DTI *Total Quality Management — A Practical Approach*, London, DTI.

DTI *The Quality Gurus What Can They Do For Your Company?*, London, DTI.

DTI *Quality Circles*, London, DTI.

EMPLOYMENT DEPARTMENT (1991) *Investing in People — The Route*, London, Employment Department.

References

ENGINEERING COUNCIL (1992) *Quality Assurance of Engineering Education and Training*, London, Engineering Council, November.

HEFCE QUALITY ASSESSMENT DIVISION (1993) *Assessors Handbook*, Bristol, HEFCE, October.

HMSO (1991) *Education and Training for the 21st Century*, London, HMSO.

MARSH, J. (1993) *The Quality Tool Kit*, Bedford, IFS Ltd.

MILLER, J., DOWER, A. and INNISS, S. (1992) *Improving Quality in Further Education*, Ware, Hartfordshire, Consultants at Work.

MILLER, J. and INNISS, S. (1990) *Improving Quality in Further Education — A Guide for Middle Managers*, Ware, Hartfordshire, Consultants at Work.

MILLER, J. and INNISS, S. (Eds) (1992) *Improving Quality*, Ware, Hartfordshire, Consultants at Work.

PORTER, M.E. (1985) *Competitive Advantage*, New York, The Free Press.

SALLIS, E. and HINGLEY, P. (1991) *College Quality Assurance Systems*, Coombe Lodge, Staff College.

SANDWELL COLLEGE (1991) *The Applicability of BS5750 to College Operations*, Sandwell, June.

Index